THE WRITING APP HANDBOOK

HOW TO CHOOSE THE BEST APP FOR FICTION AND NONFICTION WRITING

M.L. RONN

Published by Author Level Up LLC.

Edition 1, Version 3.0

Cover Design by Pixelstudio.

Covert Art © EinsteinTH / Depositphotos.

Editing by BZ Hercules.

Special thank you to the following people on Patreon who supported this book: Zhade Barnet, Stephen Frans, Michael Guishard, Jon Howard, Beth Jackson, Megan Mong, Lynda Washington, and Etta Welk.

Some links in this book contain affiliate links. If you purchase books and services through these links, I receive a small commission at no cost to you. You are under no obligation to use these links, but thank you if you do!

For more helpful writing tips and advice, subscribe to the Author Level Up YouTube channel: www.youtube.com/authorlevelup.

CONTENTS

Introduction vii

IMPORTANT THINGS TO THINK ABOUT

The Battle of the Versions: Desktop, Mobile, and Browser-Based Writing Apps 3
Writing App Pricing 6
Key Writing App Features 9

DESIGN

App Aesthetics: How Does It Look? 13
The Binder 27
Dark Mode and Color Styles 32
Content Templates 36
Customizable Toolbars 39
Customizable Backgrounds 41
Privacy Settings 43

OUTLINING AND RESEARCH

General Outlining Tools 49
Corkboard 52
Character, Setting, and Item Management 57
Timelines 62
Features for Getting Research Into Your Novel 65

ORGANIZATION

"Smart" DOC/DOCX Importing and Chapter Splitting   69

Search   72

THE WRITING EXPERIENCE

Text Zooming   81

Typewriter Mode   83

Writing in Multiple Tabs and/or Windows   85

Page View   91

Word Count Tracking and Statistics   92

Comments and Tracked Changes   96

THE FORMATTING EXPERIENCE

The Most Important Formats to Export   101

E-book Formatting   103

Paperback Formatting   109

Backing Up Your Work   113

THE HALL OF FAME: MOST INNOVATIVE WRITING APP FEATURES

Atticus: The All-in-One Approach   121

Dabble Writer: ProWritingAid Integration   124

Google Docs: The OG in Simultaneous Collaboration   125

Papyrus Author: Tracked Changes   126

Scrivener: Assisted Feature Search   127

Scrivener: Composition Mode   129

Scrivener: Linguistic Focus   131

Ulysses: Multiple Windows and Tabs at the Same Time   134

Ulysses: Style Exchange   135
Microsoft Word (and Google Docs): Macros   137

The Writing App of the Future: What Features   139
Will It Have?
Find Your Perfect Writing App With This   146
Free Tool
Read Next: The Indie Author Strategy Guide   147

Meet M.L. Ronn   149
More Books by M.L. Ronn   151

INTRODUCTION

When it comes to writing, many experts agree that war metaphors are appropriate. You're at war with words, with the page, and with yourself. Like any warrior, you must choose your weapon wisely.

Your writing app is the most important weapon in your arsenal. Get it right, and you'll become insanely productive, save time and effort, and write more. Get it wrong, and you will waste weeks, if not months of your writing career fighting with technology.

I chose the wrong weapon in 2010 and paid a serious price. I had just graduated from college and was working a crappy job in the insurance industry as a claims adjuster. Student loans were half my paycheck. I dreamed of becoming a writer, but the only tool I could afford was Microsoft Word because I was still stretching out the remainder of my student discount for Microsoft Office. I can't tell you how many hours I spent arguing with it over minor formatting issues.

One day, Word won the war. I woke up after a long night's writing session, only to find that all the words I wrote the previous day had vanished into the ether. I wanted to cry.

I was done with Word. I started searching for an alternative writing app. Even in 2010, there were many choices, but I discovered an app called Scrivener. It had everything I needed—outlining support, a split-screen writing feature (which I thought was so cool at the time), a distraction-free mode, and, best of all, a word count tracker.

There was only one problem: it cost $35. Like I said, I was broke.

I worked overtime answering phones and I sacrificed a couple of eating-out meals to afford the app. Almost immediately, I doubled my word counts because Scrivener did all the hard work. All I had to do was show up and write. Fast-forward 11 years and 60 books, and I can confidently say that I would not be half as prolific without Scrivener.

This book is not an endorsement of Scrivener—or any writing app for that matter. Instead, it's a recommendation that you find the writing app that works best for *you* and your career. When you do, amazing things will happen, just like they did for me.

Your writing app is the most important decision you will make early in your career. If you haven't found the "perfect one," it's okay. This book will help.

Why I'm Qualified to Write a Book About Writing Apps

As I wrote before, I'm the author of over 60 books of science fiction and fantasy and self-help books for writers at the time of this writing. I built my writing career while working a demanding career in insurance, raising a family, and attending law school classes in the evenings. I write five to ten books per year, sometimes more.

I discovered by accident that I have a knack for writing

apps. I have a YouTube channel called "Author Level Up" that has over 35,000 subscribers at the time of this writing. On a whim, I released a video series on how to use Scrivener. It blew up overnight. Suddenly, people asked me to do reviews of more writing apps, and I obliged.

Several years later, my writing app reviews videos on YouTube have a combined 400,000 views.

I've had the pleasure of experimenting with almost every major writing app on the market. I know them well and what makes them different. I've also gotten to know writing app developers and chatted with them about their challenges.

I hope to pass the knowledge I've learned to you so that you can find your dream app.

I've made a name for myself in reviewing writing apps because my subscribers enjoy my "nitty-gritty" personality. I'm not afraid to go in-depth so that viewers can understand every part of the app.

I've spoken about writing to crowds of over 1,000 people: 20 Books Vegas and multiple Writer's Digest conferences. I've also been a featured guest on major writing shows such as "The Creative Penn." I'm frequently asked to do demos of writing apps, which I enjoy.

I won the writing war, and it's all because I chose my weapons wisely. I want to help you do the same.

How to Use This Book

This book is not a tutorial for any writing app. As I stated before, it is not an endorsement for any writing app.

This book is also not an app review book. If I reviewed apps, this book would quickly become obsolete.

Instead, think of this book as a consumer's guide. I will walk you through the major features of most writing apps on the market today, including some features you may not be aware of. While the apps themselves may change, features are forever. My goal is to help you understand the features to figure out which ones are important to you.

I like to think of the writing app process as similar to buying a car. When buying a car, you:

- research all the features and customizations of the cars you're considering
- determine which features are your deal breakers
- find the most comfortable "fit"

Writing apps are no different. Just as you'd want to buy a car that suits your lifestyle, you also want a writing app that conforms to the way you write. Many drivers buy cars because of the features too—after all, you're going to be using that car a lot and spending a lot of time in it. You're also going to be spending a lot of time in your writing app, so it better be comfortable. And most importantly, car consumers are price conscious, and so are writers.

Use the information in this guide to help you become a more informed consumer. You can also use the information in this guide to suggest features for the writing app you already use. Nothing motivates developers better than a bunch of customers asking for a new feature.

In the **Important Things to Think About** section, I cover a few items that you should know before buying a writing app.

In the **Key Writing App Features** section, I cover key selling points of the hottest writing apps on the market. I've organized the features by:

- Design

- Outlining & Research
- Organization
- The Writing Experience
- The Formatting Experience
- Backing Up Your Work

In each part, I describe how the features work. I also include screenshots so you can see the features in action.

In the **Hall of Fame** section, I discuss features that are so unique and game-changing that they're worth knowing about. These features are only available on one specific app, but they're beacons of innovation that should be celebrated for pushing writing app technology forward.

And finally, in **The Writing App of the Future,** I offer some thoughts about what I believe the writing app of the future may look like.

A Quick Word on the Writing Apps Included in This Book

There are many apps out there. Some are outside the scope of this book.

I believe that writers who are serious about their careers should invest in professional tools designed for them.

My main requirement when including apps in this book was that the app had to be designed specifically for authors and novelists.

The exceptions are general-use writing apps like Microsoft Word, Apple's Pages, and OpenOffice; while these apps aren't designed for (specifically) writers, writers use them because they often come pre-installed on new computers or because they are free. Many writers use Google Docs too, so it also passed the test.

If the app's main function is something else (like editing, formatting, note-taking, and so on), then I did not consider that to be a "writing app" for this book. Examples include Evernote, Grammarly, Day One, ProWritingAid, Vellum, and so on.

For example, Evernote was not built for novels, even though you can technically write one in it. That said, novel writing is not why Evernote was created; it was created for note-taking and helping people get more organized. For that reason, writers who write their books in Evernote will face significant problems.

The test is the following question: "If I said I wrote books on X app, would people think I was crazy?"

I know that there are a lot of people who write their books on unconventional platforms, and that's great. Do whatever works best for you. However, this book doesn't focus on unconventional apps because it's too difficult to do comparisons. I want you to find the best fit, and you're more likely to find that fit with a dedicated writing app.

Also, it's worth noting that writing apps (and developers) aren't infallible to life, death, and unfortunate circumstances. Sometimes people die or move on to other things, and writing apps die. I'll do my best to keep this book up-to-date every few years, but when in doubt, keep reading for a tool that will help you stay up-to-date (that's easier for me to update).

And finally,

Also, a few disclaimers:

- Always check to verify that a feature exists in the operating system you use. For example, just because something exists in a Mac version doesn't guarantee it on the Windows version. I do my best to call out any differences, but make sure you still do your research. What you buy is your responsibility.

- Everything in this book is current as of the time it was written. App developers of course release new features all the time. Have a little grace with this book in that regard.
- I don't cover mobile writing apps in this book. That's because right now, there aren't that many good ones. Furthermore, my testing found that there is not a good Android writing app at the time of this writing—at least, not anything that approaches what iOS users have. So I left mobile apps out because I didn't want this book to be a complete Apple lovefest.
- I don't own all the writing apps listed in this book, so I had to rely on what I could find with free trials for screenshots.
- This book contains examples from (mostly) Mac and Windows apps. This is mainly because these are operating systems I use regularly. I'm not familiar with Linux, though I do have it. Keep reading for a free companion tool I developed that is more diverse and represents all operating systems more fairly.

An Alternative Way to Viewing Images

This book contains a lot of images. If you can't view them well on your device, go to www.authorlevelup.com/handbookimages so you can see them in high-resolution.

I Also Built a Free Tool for You

Because I want you to find the best match, I put together the Writing App Database: it's a detailed web page that lists the features of all the major writing apps side-by-side so you can compare them. You can filter by operating system too. (There is more diverse representation too!)

You'll even find links to where you can download the apps.

If you don't see your favorite app on the list, let me know, and I'd be happy to include it.

The database is free, but you're certainly welcome to drop a donation in the tip jar if you feel so moved to do so!

You can find the Writing App Database at www.authorlevelup.com/writingapps.

My sincerest hope is that this book (and the database) will help you find your weapon in this crazy war called writing. When you find it, you'll know.

Happy writing, and happy app shopping!

M.L. Ronn
July 1, 2021
Des Moines, Iowa

IMPORTANT THINGS TO
THINK ABOUT

THE BATTLE OF THE VERSIONS: DESKTOP, MOBILE, AND BROWSER-BASED WRITING APPS

Writing apps come in three different versions: desktop, mobile (and/or tablet), and browser-based. No writing app I've tested offers all three.

Desktop apps give you a smorgasbord of features and the most flexibility. There's almost nothing in the writing process that they cannot do. You also do not have to have an internet connection to use them.

The downside to desktop apps is that you have to be in front of your computer to use them.

Mobile writing apps let you write on your phone or tablet. Some desktop apps have desktop *and* mobile versions so you can sync between them. The advantage of mobile apps is that you can write anywhere. They're also cheaper than their desktop counterparts. You also do not need an internet connection to use them.

The downside to mobile apps is that you have to write with your thumbs, which may be a non-starter if you have repetitive stress injuries or issues with your hands, arms, or wrists. You can invest in a Bluetooth keyboard to help you type, but you have to carry that around with you, and that may not be worth the hassle.

Mobile writing apps exist to help you write on the go, and that's about it. You'll find that they're severely lacking compared to their desktop counterparts. You can't use tracked changes when you're editing, for example, and formatting is impossible. (Though Microsoft Word's mobile app is the notable exception to this—it's about as close to full-functional as you can get).

Another issue with mobile apps is syncing. They sync with services like Dropbox, OneDrive and iCloud. If you are in a location with a bad cell signal or Wi-Fi, you may not be able to sync your versions, so always make sure you sync before you walk out the door! Otherwise, you'll be doing what I had to do as I was writing this chapter in a pizzeria—wait *forever* for it to sync, and hope for the best.

Some users also report trouble getting sync functionality to work. It's not always the developer's fault; sometimes you're at the whim of cloud service providers too. I am an avid mobile user and I've only encountered a handful of issues with syncing. All of them were resolved. But it can be frustrating when your words are locked on your phone or your desktop and you can't access them on the device you need them on.

Browser-based writing apps are the newest type of writing app, and they only require a browser and an Internet connection to use. You can write in any browser, which means (in theory) that you can write on any device with an Internet connection. Browser-based apps are also cross-platform: Windows, Mac, and Linux users can use them and get the same results. Browser-based apps also have the advantage of supporting collaboration, so multiple authors can work on a project at the same time, if the developer chooses to implement that functionality.

The downside to browser-based apps is that they just can't

match the features of most desktop apps because they're limited by whatever requirements the browser places on them.

Also, a browser-based app won't work (well) on mobile devices until its developer actively supports mobile devices.

You also have to beware of security issues with browser-based apps. You're more susceptible to hacking attacks because all someone needs are your username and password to access your work-in-progress. Also, you don't know what security protocols the developer is taking, so the entire network could be exploited, resulting in your losing access to your work or losing it altogether. At the time of this writing, browser-based writing apps are a Wild West. Developers *say* they are taking proper security measures, but unless you're a developer and can gauge the accuracy of their claims for yourself, you never really know.

And finally, browser-based apps are more likely to be subscription-based, which means once you stop paying, you can no longer use the service. (Some desktop and mobile writing apps are subscription-based too, but we'll talk about that later).

Which type of writing app should you use? It depends on your needs.

I use a mixture of desktop and mobile apps. That works best for me because I'm frequently on the go, and I'm wary of browser-based app security at the moment.

You'll want to weigh the pros and cons carefully, especially if a subscription fee is at stake.

WRITING APP PRICING

Let's talk about pricing because this is always a touchy topic in the writing community.

There are five pricing models in the writing app space: free, freemium, flat fee, subscription-based, and pay-what-you-want.

In a free model, the writing app is free, but you're invited to donate to support the developer. yWriter is an example of free software.

In a freemium model, you can use the app for free with some limitations, but you can purchase a premium license to remove those limitations. Dabble Writer and Papyrus Author both have freemium models, with the premium part being subscription-based.

Flat fee models let you purchase the entire app with no limitations in exchange for a onetime fee. You then have to pay every time a new version is released. Scrivener uses a flat fee model.

Subscription-based writing apps allow access to the app in exchange for a monthly or yearly subscription. Ulysses operates under a subscription model.

Authors just don't like subscription-based models. At all. I can't tell you how many people who comment on my YouTube channel that they will *never* buy a subscription-based app.

Why? Well, for Mac users, a certain app used to be a flat fee but then switched to subscriptions, which angered its user base (cough, Ulysses, cough). Right, wrong, or indifferent, Ulysses's developers made the decision they felt they needed to sustain their business. And, right, wrong, or indifferent, some of its users vehemently disagreed with *how* the developer did it.

The sentiment makes sense. Before the advent of subscriptions, writing apps cost under $75, usually much less. Now, people are being asked to pay that (or more) per year.

Writing doesn't make money for many authors, especially not in the beginning. With all the money that writers have to pay to produce their books and establish their careers, it's no wonder writers are hesitant to pay subscriptions.

That said, if you look at my Writing App Database and filter away the outliers, the most expensive subscription at the time of this writing is around $15 per month or $180 per year. If you think about other professions, they pay way more than that for their tools. A professional artist pays more than $180 per year in brushes, canvases, and paint supplies per year. A musician probably pays more than $180 per year in instrument repairs, maintenance, and accessories. Contractors, attorneys, and even insurance agents pay many more times than that for their tools. Even though we don't like subscriptions, we've got it pretty good.

Developers who support the subscription model claim that it helps keep cash coming into the business. They also like subscriptions because they can use that money to update the app more frequently with updates that users want. In the hands of the right developers, I believe this is true. For example, the team behind Ulysses routinely releases an update with new features every three to four months. Whether you like the subscription model or not, they should be commended for that, and they've set a proper standard for what subscription users should expect.

In the wrong hands, subscriptions are a bad experience that leaves authors feeling like they were cheated.

If you don't like subscriptions, then you've made your decision; you don't have to finish reading this chapter.

If you are open to paying a subscription, consider:

- the value of the features you get compared to similar apps
- how frequently the developer releases updates
- what other writers are saying about the app
- the app's track record and how long it has been around
- how much money you are making from your writing and how sustainable the subscription is

As long as you understand what you're getting into, there's nothing wrong with subscriptions as long as the developer is reasonable about it and upholds their end of the promise.

Finally, we have the pay-what-you-want model, which is pretty straightforward. The developer offers the app at a minimum price (say $5) and you can pay the minimum or any amount over that. Pay-what-you-want models are rare at the time of this writing, but they do exist.

KEY WRITING APP FEATURES

DESIGN

APP AESTHETICS: HOW DOES IT LOOK?

A writing app's design is an important decision because it makes the first impression. You want a design that you will be comfortable looking at for a long time. While it's true that some writing apps don't "look" the best but work just fine, it's a bonus if you like the design.

WYSIWYG or Markdown?

The first item for consideration is whether you prefer What You See Is What You Get (WYSIWYG) text processing or Markdown.

WYSIWYG text processing is traditional and probably what you're used to. You type words onto a digital page, and when you print that page or export it to another format, it looks the same as how you typed it.

Microsoft Word is the most iconic example of WYSIWYG:

WYSIWYG editor example. Microsoft Word (Windows). View in high-resolution at www.authorlevelup.com/handbookimages.

Scrivener is a continuation of this school.

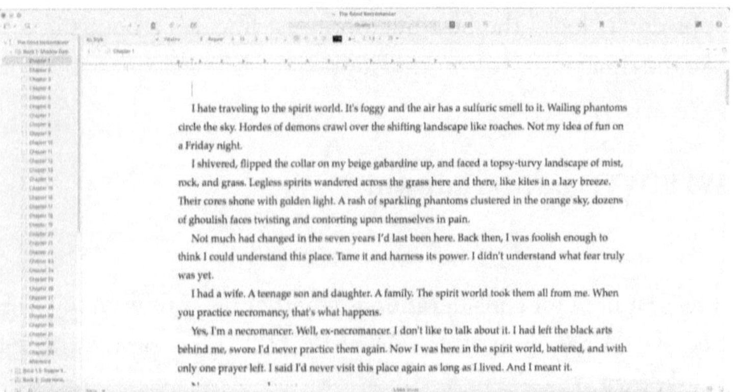

Another WYSIWYG editor example. Scrivener (Mac). View in high-resolution at www.authorlevelup.com/handbookimages.

Even Apple's minimalistic app, Pages, is WYSIWYG, though it has a different aesthetic look.

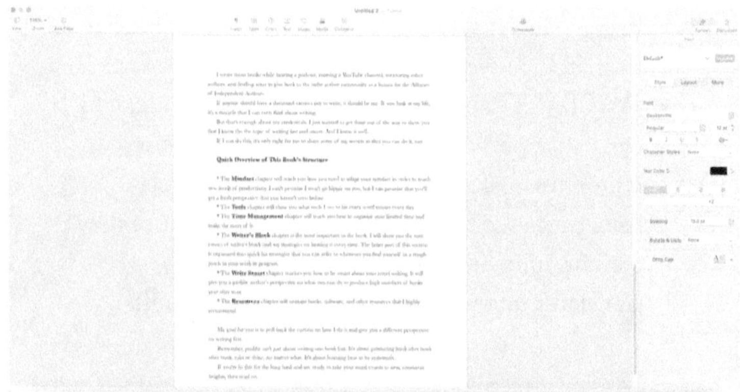

Pages' WYSIWYG editor. (Mac). View in high-resolution at www.authorlevelup.com/handbookimages.

With WYSIWYG editing, users want assurance that what they type and how they type it is reproduced when they export it. This is part of WYSIWYG's charm, but also part of its danger. When something doesn't look right in a WYSIWYG app, you can spend a lot of effort trying to fix it.

The pros of WYSIWYG software:

- Pleasant look.
- Intuitive.
- You don't need to be techy to create respectable-looking text.

The cons of WYSIWYG are:

- Formatting can be an exercise in frustration.
- What you see isn't always what you get.
- WYSIWYG apps usually store files in a proprietary

format (such as .DOCX), which can make it a hassle to switch between programs.

- WYSIWYG apps can contain "bloated" code, which can cause performance issues or other unforeseen issues during formatting. Code-savvy people sometimes scoff at WYSIWYG apps because they contain unnecessary code. This *sometimes* translates into making your life more difficult.

A Markdown editor supports Markdown, which is a markup language designed for formatting text in a text editor. I've always thought it is confusing to call Markdown a markup language, but I digress...

The big difference with Markdown is that, whereas a WYSIWYG app assures you of how the final document will look before you print it, Markdown assures you of what the document will look like *after* you print it.

When working with text, WYSIWYG users are used to visiting a toolbar and clicking a "Style" for Heading 1, a "B" for bold, and "Insert Link" for web links.

The result is:

Formatting elements at work in a WYSIWYG app. Microsoft Word (Mac). View in high-resolution at www.authorlevelup. com/handbookimages.

With Markdown, you use special symbols to accomplish the same purpose:

- # in front of text that is Heading 1
- ** in front and behind text that is bolded
- [ ] around links

This is what that same text looks like in Markdown:

Markdown example. iA Writer (Mac). View in high-resolution
at www.authorlevelup.com/handbookimages.

In theory, when you export the Markdown file, it should
look identical to the text in the WYSIWYG editor. The benefit
is that you can format Markdown as you write it without having
to take your fingers off the keyboard, so once you understand it,
you can write faster because you're formatting as you go.

However, the visual design is much different from Markdown. Take Ulysses—its style is drastically different from the
WYSIWYG editors shown previously:

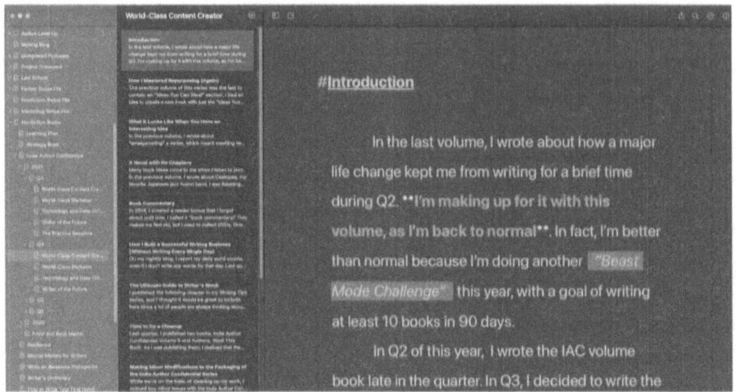

Ulysses (Mac). View in high-resolution at www.authorlevelup.
com/handbookimages.

Many people remark that Markdown looks like computer code, and they're right. The Markdown language was originally designed as an alternative to HTML. Markdown looks best against a dark background because it makes the text easier to see. When I write Markdown, I feel as if I'm a computer programmer. However, Markdown is more useful because unlike HTML, you don't have to worry about all those angle brackets. It's cleaner.

The benefit of Markdown is that you're working with text files, which are easier to work with than the proprietary files of WYSIWYG editors, so there's less bloat. For this reason, Markdown software is noticeably "zippier." Also, because you don't have to worry about toolbars and other intricate features, you can focus primarily on the text.

Another benefit of Markdown is the same benefit of HTML: consistency. Despite the name of a WYSIWYG editor, you're not always guaranteed to get what you see. With Markdown, the results are better. So yes, while you have to adapt to using hashtags and other symbols around your text, you can be reasonably assured that your work will look the same on most devices when you export it. Markdown apps can export to Microsoft Word, HTML, and even ePUB while also supporting direct uploads to sites like WordPress and Medium. Their exporting capability allows you to see instantaneous previews of how your text will look across different formats. For example, Ulysses gives you different previews with the click of a button. The only thing I changed on each of these was the preview type:

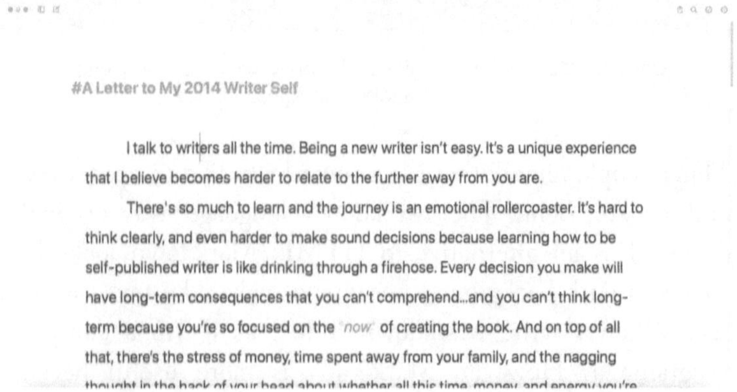

Ulysses's main writing editor (Mac). This is what the chapter looks like in Markdown. View in high-resolution at www.authorlevelup.com/handbookimages.

A Letter to My 2014 Writer Self

I talk to writers all the time. Being a new writer isn't easy. It's a unique experience that I believe becomes harder to relate to the further away from you are.

There's so much to learn and the journey is an emotional rollercoaster. It's hard to think clearly, and even harder to make sound decisions because learning how to be self-published writer is like drinking through a firehose. Every decision you make will have long-term consequences that you can't comprehend… and you can't think long-term because you're so focused on the now of creating the book. And on top of all that, there's the stress of money, time spent away from your family, and the nagging thought in the back of your head about whether all this time, money, and energy you're spending on a dream is going to work out.

Yet new writers are endlessly optimistic. It's a beautifully complicated, emotional and optimistic time to be alive.

This got me thinking about what advice I would give to my 2014 self. If I could travel back in time to give writing advice to myself, what would I say?

Dear Michael,

Greetings from 2021! Though we are separated by seven years, I understand you very well because I am you.

Congratulations on writing your first book, How to Be Bad. It was an amazing feat to pull off, but you did it.

I regret to inform you that it won't sell very well, despite your optimism. In fact, you'll rebrand the book in a few years and it still won't sell.

But I have good news: as I write this letter, I've just started production on my fifty-fourth book, and it will probably sell pretty well!

It won't be until 2020 until you see the type of success you expect, and even then you won't be making a living. But you'll be proud.

If I may, I'd like to give you some advice.

1. Now that you've written your first book, you know the territory of a writer. It will never get easier to write a book, but you'll improve your confidence.
2. Keep reading voraciously and never stop. It will be difficult to balance writing, reading, business, and marketing, but it will be vital to find harmony between them.
3. You'll win (almost) every time you follow your instinct.
4. The more you write, the more you will succeed.
5. Learn how to use Amazon and Facebook ads without ignoring them at first, for God's sake!

Keep doing what you're doing. There will be many nights where you'll question whether this will work out. There will be times when you feel like it won't work out, especially when you publish book after book and don't see the financial numbers you'd like to see.

But your experience is valuable and people all over the world will be watching you every day to see how you are doing and what you think about things related to the writing life.

Keep documenting your journey and keep finding ways to connect with your readers.

Sincerely,

Future Michael

I don't think that letter really scratches the surface of deep advice, and that brings me what I truly learned in this exercise: you can't really skip past being new. No advice can truly help you. You're going to do what you're going to do, and if you're lucky, one day you'll wake up, realize that you've made enough mistakes and start truly seeking advice that will be meaningful. You'll be frustrated at that point, but you'll find the advice that work best for you. This didn't happen for me until early 2015.

The key is that hopefully you haven't made career-ending mistakes, such as signing a bad contract, falling prey to a scam or getting your publishing accounts canceled because you used bad judgment with a marketing technique. If you didn't do any of those things, you're golden. If you did, you may not have a career.

Ulysses's preview mode (Mac). This is what the chapter will look like if exported to a Rich Text File (.RTF). View in high-resolution at www.authorlevelup.com/handbookimages.

A Letter to My 2014 Writer Self

I talk to writers all the time. Being a new writer isn't easy. It's a unique experience that I believe becomes harder to relate to the further away from you are.

There's so much to learn and the journey is an emotional rollercoaster. It's hard to think clearly, and even harder to make sound decisions because learning how to be self-published writer is like drinking through a firehose. Every decision you make will have long-term consequences that you can't comprehend…and you can't think long-term because you're so focused on the now of creating the book. And on top of all that, there's the stress of money, time spent away from your family, and the nagging thought in the back of your head about whether all this time, money, and energy you're spending on a dream is going to work out.

Yet new writers are endlessly optimistic. It's a beautifully complicated, emotional and optimistic time to be alive.

This got me thinking about what advice I would give to my 2014 self. If I could travel back in time to give writing advice to myself, what would I say?

Dear Michael,

Greetings from 2021! Though we are separated by seven years, I

Ulysses's preview mode (Mac). This is what the chapter will look like if exported to HTML. View in high-resolution at www.authorlevelup.com/handbookimages.

A LETTER TO MY 2014 WRITER SELF

I talk to writers all the time. Being a new writer isn't easy. It's a unique experience that I believe becomes harder to relate to the further away from you are.

There's so much to learn and the journey is an emotional rollercoaster. It's hard to think clearly, and even harder to make sound decisions because learning how to be self-published writer is like drinking through a firehose. Every decision you make will have long-term consequences that you can't comprehend…and you can't think long-term because you're so focused on the *now* of creating the book. And on top of all that, there's the stress of money, time spent away from your family, and the nagging thought in the back of your head about whether all this time, money, and energy you're spending on a *dream* is going to work out.

Yet new writers are endlessly optimistic. It's a beautifully complicated, emotional and optimistic time to be alive.

This got me thinking about what advice I would give to my 2014 self. If I could travel back in time to give writing advice to myself, what would I say?

Dear Michael,

Greetings from 2021! Though we are separated by seven years, I understand you very well because I am you.

Congratulations on writing your first book, *How to Be Bad*. It was an amazing feat to pull off, but you did it.

I regret to inform you that it won't sell very well, despite your optimism. In fact, you'll rebrand the book in a few years and it still won't sell.

But I have good news: as I write this letter, I've just started production on my fifty-fourth book, and it will probably sell pretty well!

It won't be until 2020 until you see the type of success you expect, and even then you won't be making a living. But you'll be proud.

If I may, I'd like to give you some advice.

1. Now that you've written your first book, you know the territory of a writer. It will never get easier to write a book, but you'll improve your confidence.

Ulysses's preview mode (Mac). This is what the chapter will look like if exported to ePUB. View in high-resolution at www.authorlevelup.com/handbookimages.

It takes some getting used to the visual aesthetic of Markdown, but once you understand its power, you can be more just as productive as you would in a WYSIWYG editor, maybe more.

A downside to Markdown is that while formatting is smoother, *book formatting* isn't so smooth. There's a difference between formatting text for HTML, PDF, or Word, and formatting it for e-books. At the time of this writing, Markdown apps still lag behind their WYSIWYG counterparts in e-book formatting, and apps like Ulysses require users to understand code such as cascading style sheets (CSS) to refine formatting for e-books. That intimidates a lot of people, and for good reason.

Paperback formatting is impossible with Markdown apps; don't even think about it. This alone is a major turn-off for writers. (But if you use a dedicated book formatting app like Vellum, then it doesn't matter.)

The pros of Markdown:

- Simpler interface with great dark modes.

- More flexibility when writing your text.
- Zippier app speed and performance.
- Easier distraction-free writing.
- Easy to learn if you invest the time.
- Smaller files since you're dealing with text files.

The cons:

- There is a learning curve, even though it's not difficult.
- It scares most non-techy people.
- Book formatting is lackluster.

Whether you're writing on a computer app, your phone, or your desktop, you will encounter either WYSIWYG or Markdown editors.

Modern, Minimalist, or Old-school?

What about the design of the app itself? Writing app designs are always a work-in-progress, often tied to the developments of operating systems (at least on Windows and Mac OS).

Many writing apps are sleek and easy to look at, with attractive color schemes designed for long writing sessions. I call that the "modern look."

Living Writer is a new-school, browser-based app with a modern look. (Web-Based). View in high-resolution at www. authorlevelup.com/handbookimages.

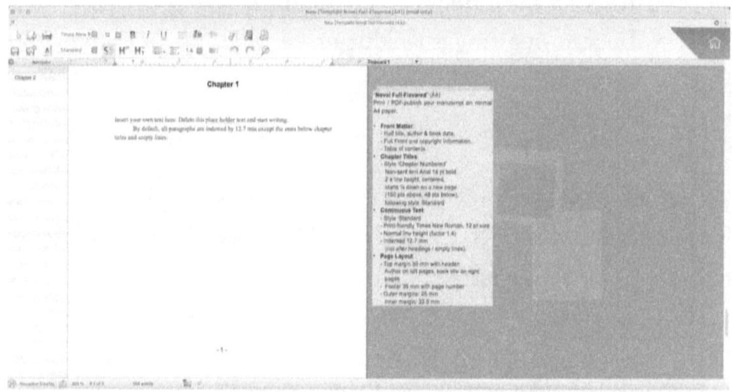

Papyrus Author also has a modern look that is slightly more retro. (Mac). View in high-resolution at www.authorlevelup. com/handbookimages.

Other writing apps are more minimalist. They exist mainly to help writers minimize distractions and focus on the words.

Bibisco takes a minimalistic approach. (Windows). View in high-resolution at www.authorlevelup.com/handbookimages.

One of my favorite old-school designs is an app called Writer's Café, which is designed to look like an old-school Windows operating system. It's an operating system within an operating system!

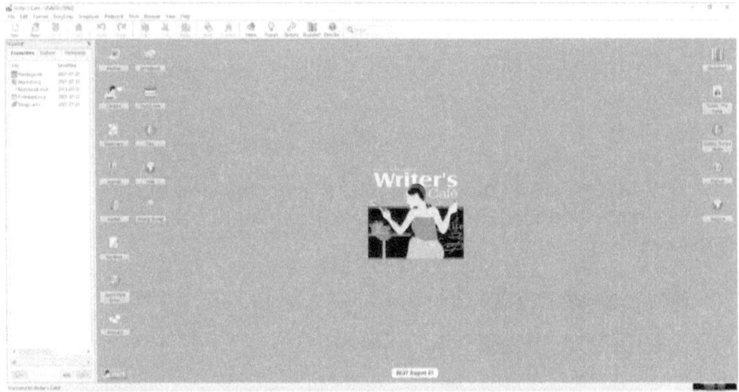

Writer's Café is about as old-school a design you can find. (Windows). View in high-resolution at www.authorlevelup. com/handbookimages.

I happen to like the old-school designs; they remind me that despite how far we've come, writing apps haven't truly changed that much. Ultimately, you're typing into a text processor, manipulating it, and printing (exporting) it. Sometimes we get so wrapped up in the "new" that we forget how functional the "old" is!

I also find that Windows apps have an old-school look despite having advanced operating systems like Windows 10 and 11. Something about even the most cutting-edge Windows writing apps always looks outdated to me, but maybe that's because I prefer Mac apps. Some people don't mind the Windows look; others can't stand it.

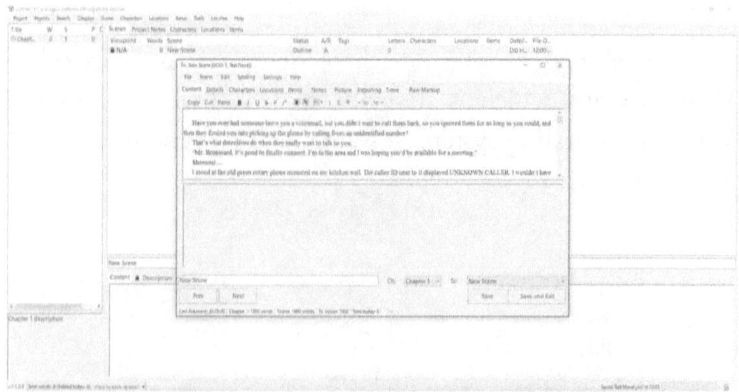

yWriter has an old-school feel. (Windows). View in high-resolution at www.authorlevelup.com/handbookimages.

Remember, you're the one who will be staring at the screen. Pick an app with a design that's most suitable for your preferences.

THE BINDER

Writing apps differ wildly, but the one feature almost all of them have in common is the binder. The binder is a strip on the left-hand side of the screen that houses all of your chapters, research, and other documents.

Binders typify the "modern" writing app because they let you store *all* related documents in the same place without causing problems. When it's time to export your book, simply select the documents you want to export. You can easily add, edit, and delete documents with ease, and there's usually a recycling bin just in case you accidentally delete something.

Some binders allow you to change the icons of your documents for additional customization.

START HERE

Key Concepts

Draft

The Basics

Get Oriented

Main Interface

The Binder

The Editor

The Inspector

Synopsis & Notes

Label & Status

Bookmarks

Metadata

Snapshots

Comments & Footnotes

Composition Mode

Get Organised

Splitting the Editor

Editor View Modes

The Corkboard

The Outliner

Scrivenings

Get It Out There

Section Types

Compiling the Draft

Binder example. Scrivener (Windows) View in high-resolution at www.authorlevelup.com/handbookimages.

- Project
  - My Manuscript
  - Title Page
  - About This Template
  - Characters
    - Protagonist
    - Antagonist
  - Settings
    - Example Setting
  - Images
    - About the Images F...

Binder example. Storyist (Mac). View in high-resolution at www.authorlevelup.com/handbookimages.

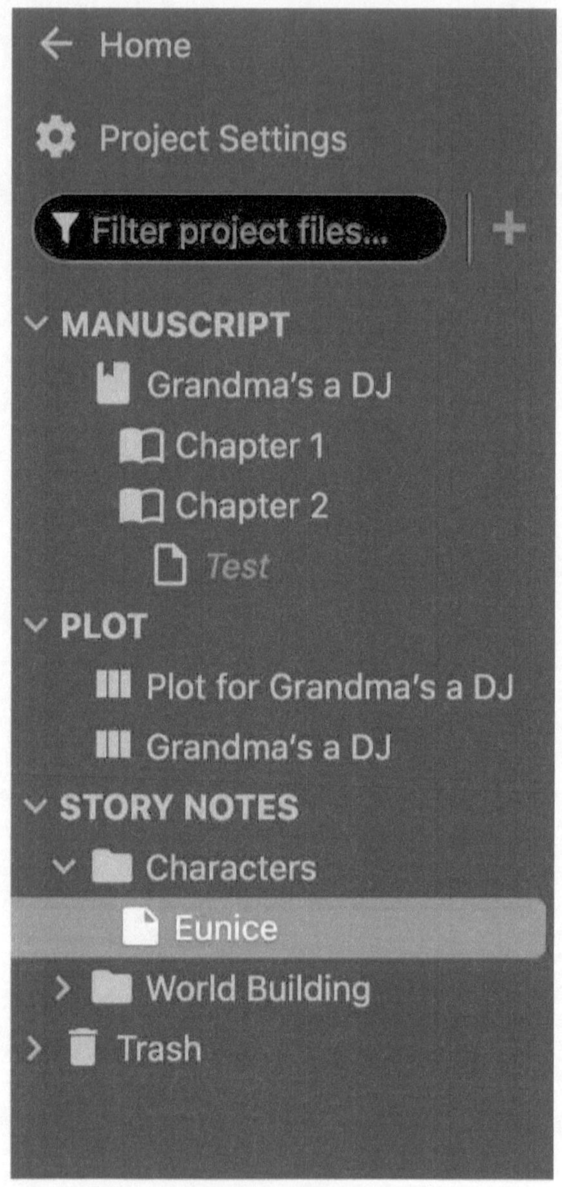

Binder example. Dabble (Web-Based). View in high-resolution at www.authorlevelup.com/handbookimages.

No matter what your writing app, you'll probably be working in a binder. The key is to find the binder that resonates most with you.

DARK MODE AND COLOR STYLES

After the overall design of a writing app, the color style is also important. There are two major choices to think about.

White Mode, Dark Mode, or Both?

Until recently (circa 2016), most writing apps defaulted to "white". This meant black text on a white background. Dark backgrounds harken back to the old-school days of computing, and not requested by consumers until recently. I *never* even heard the words "dark mode" until 2016.

With the rise of dark modes and improved screen resolutions on computers, phones, and tablets, now *everyone* wants this look.

Black is back because:

- it causes less eyestrain.
- it improves contrast and is easier to read.

- it creates a desirable color contrast, especially with unique colors.
- both Windows and Macintosh operating systems have built-in dark modes, and apps now support darker colors. iOS and Android also have dark modes.
- apps such as Gmail, Kindle, Chrome, and more support dark modes, so users are more familiar with it and have come to expect it everywhere.

Now, the writing community is crazy about dark modes. It went from an obscure feature to a key selling point for many people. It happened over just a few years.

When you look at the same app in both modes, it's easy to see why people like dark mode so much.

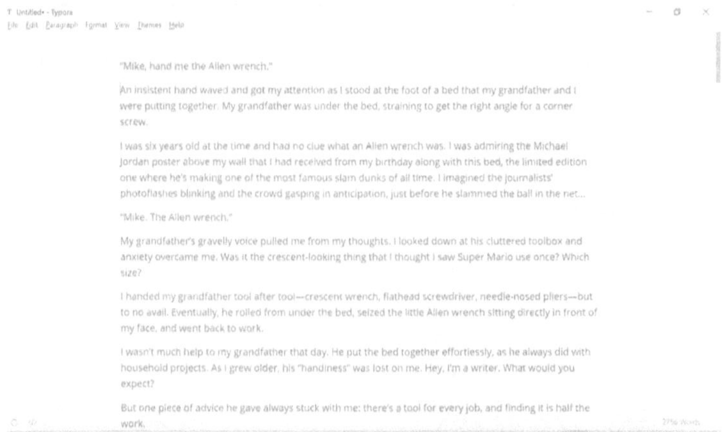

Typora in GitHub Mode (White). (Windows). View in high-resolution at www.authorlevelup.com/handbookimages.

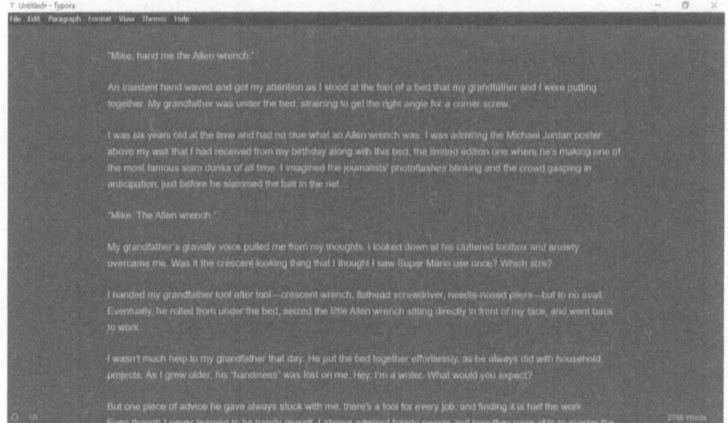

Typora in Night Mode (Dark). (Windows). View in high-resolution at www.authorlevelup.com/handbookimages.

Some people still prefer a white background, but I believe dark mode is here to stay. It's nice to be able to switch between the two when needed. For example, users may switch to dark mode at night to reduce eyestrain, but if they're writing outside on a sunny day, they'll switch to white mode because it's easier to see in direct sunlight.

In my opinion, the *only* way to use Markdown apps is in dark mode.

Which Colors Do You Like?

A few writing apps allow you to change the color theme so you can write in the comfort of a different color palette.

Apps such as Ulysses even allow users to create their styles and share them in a free marketplace.

Purple is my favorite color, so I'm always drawn to color schemes that have purple in them. Other people like solarized themes. I know one person who likes "ketchup and mustard" themes. Don't criticize it until you've tried it!

Developers can also create new "skins" or color themes easily.

The only limitation with app color schemes is what developers and users can dream of.

Are colorized writing apps a major selling point? Probably not, but I believe more apps should have them. They help writers customize their writing experience and be more comfortable in long writing sessions.

CONTENT TEMPLATES

Writing apps have many features. It's not uncommon to feel overwhelmed when booting up your new writing app for the first time.

People fall into one of two camps when they start a new app:

- They want to read the instruction documentation, watch tutorial videos, and maybe even take a paid course to learn the software better.
- They want to jump in, start using the app right away, and learn it as they go.

No matter which camp you're in, it's easy to get overwhelmed by the sheer number of features many writing apps have.

Content templates are a wonderful way for writers to get started on writing their book quickly without having to "set up" a writing app to their liking.

Want to write a novel? There's a template for that, with

your research folders, outline, character sheets, and chapters already set up. Just by seeing how the developers arranged the template, you can learn how best to use it and customize it to your taste.

Scrivener has one of the most famous templates for novels.

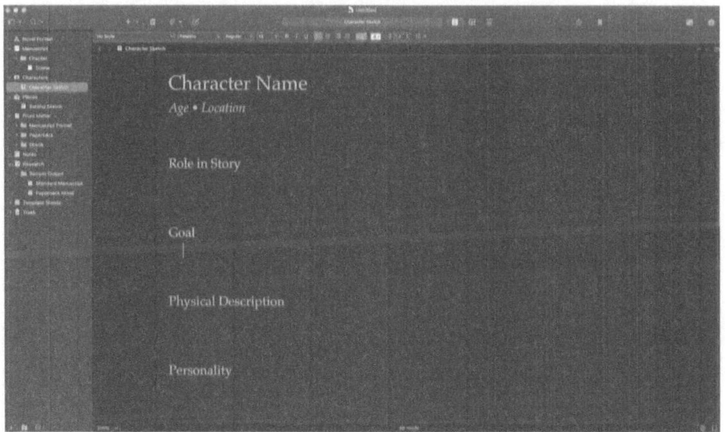

Scrivener novel template with a character sheet. (Mac). View in high-resolution at www.authorlevelup.com/handbookimages.

Other common content templates include:

- Screenplays
- Poetry
- Short stories (especially manuscript format for magazine submissions)

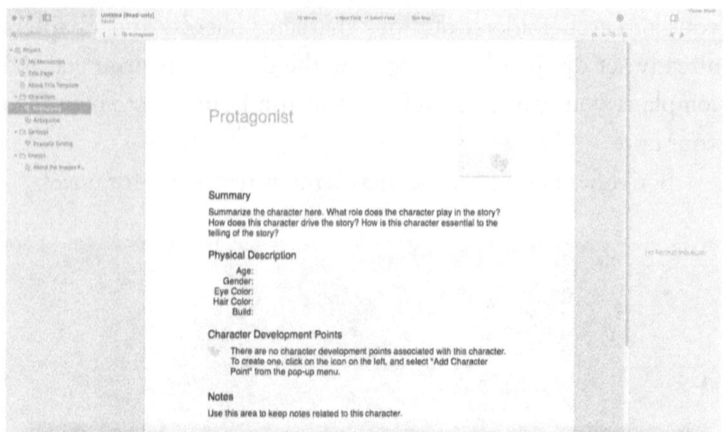

Storyist novel template with a character sheet. (Mac). View in high-resolution at www.authorlevelup.com/handbookimages.

I've done countless demos of writing apps, and the question of content templates frequently comes up, especially from authors and poets who want to go through the magazine submission process. Screenplay writers also like the structure that templates provide because they don't have to worry as much about making mistakes.

If you don't like a template, you can modify it. You can also create your own templates.

Content templates aren't just a shortcut for beginners. They're also a productivity tool. Create your own templates so that your files are set up the exact way you want them every time you start a project. Templates save you time and effort so you can spend more time writing.

CUSTOMIZABLE TOOLBARS

Many writing apps have toolbars. These toolbars rest at the top of the screen and contain icons that correspond to a certain function like font, font size, lists, or alignment.

What happens if you don't like the icons on the toolbar? What if you won't use most of them and would like to customize the toolbar with icons that you will use regularly?

Some writing apps allow this.

The most famous toolbar of all time is Microsoft Word's. It allows for flexible customization.

Microsoft Word's toolbar. (Mac). View in high-resolution at www.authorlevelup.com/handbookimages.

Most writing apps are merely a variation on this theme. Papyrus Author is a good example of this.

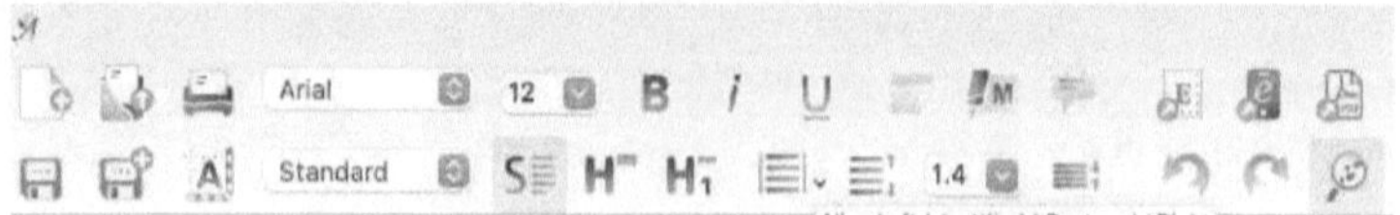

Papyrus Author's toolbar. (Mac). View in high-resolution at www.authorlevelup.com/handbookimages.

Toolbar customization is a minimalist's dream; it allows you to remove unnecessary icons so that you have only what you need.

It is also a productivity tool because you'll spend less time hunting for icons when there are fewer of them. This is uniquely a WYSIWYG problem. I've heard many people complain about how they can never seem to find anything in their writing app. Having used many apps, this is a fair criticism, especially of feature-rich ones.

Toolbar customization is often overlooked, even by writers who have been using an app for a long time. Taking a few minutes to set up your toolbar will help your writing sessions and save you effort.

CUSTOMIZABLE BACKGROUNDS

Some people don't like white backgrounds or black backgrounds. It feels boring to them, so they want to write with a more festive backdrop, like autumn leaves, a pristine beach, or a picture of their favorite cat.

Everyone has their preferences, and more power to them!

Focus Writer has a prominent customizable background feature that either speaks to you or it makes you instantly hate it. But it's the best representation of this feature in all the writing apps I reviewed.

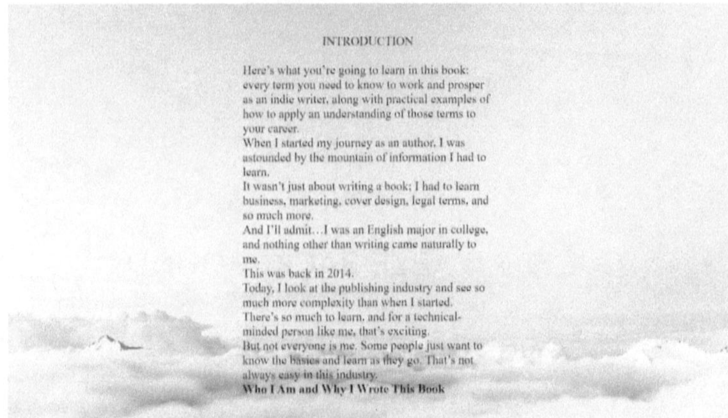

INTRODUCTION

Here's what you're going to learn in this book: every term you need to know to work and prosper as an indie writer, along with practical examples of how to apply an understanding of those terms to your career.
When I started my journey as an author, I was astounded by the mountain of information I had to learn.
It wasn't just about writing a book; I had to learn business, marketing, cover design, legal terms, and so much more.
And I'll admit…I was an English major in college, and nothing other than writing came naturally to me.
This was back in 2014.
Today, I look at the publishing industry and see so much more complexity than when I started.
There's so much to learn, and for a technical-minded person like me, that's exciting.
But not everyone is me. Some people just want to know the basics and learn as they go. That's not always easy in this industry.
Who I Am and Why I Wrote This Book

Writing on a blue sky background. FocusWriter (Windows). View in high-resolution at www.authorlevelup.com/handbookimages.

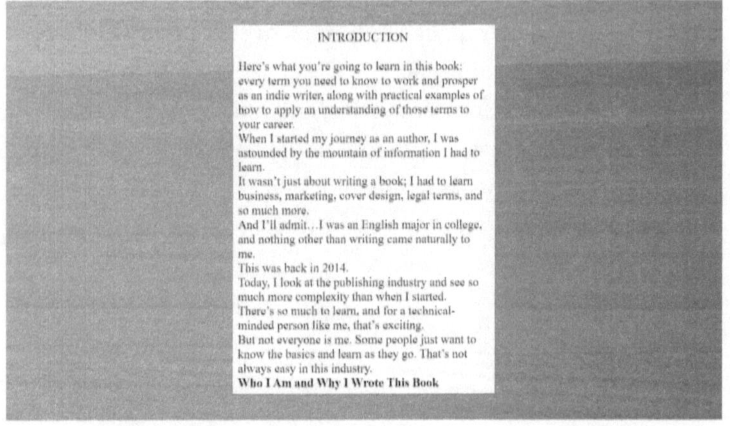

INTRODUCTION

Here's what you're going to learn in this book: every term you need to know to work and prosper as an indie writer, along with practical examples of how to apply an understanding of those terms to your career.
When I started my journey as an author, I was astounded by the mountain of information I had to learn.
It wasn't just about writing a book; I had to learn business, marketing, cover design, legal terms, and so much more.
And I'll admit…I was an English major in college, and nothing other than writing came naturally to me.
This was back in 2014.
Today, I look at the publishing industry and see so much more complexity than when I started.
There's so much to learn, and for a technical-minded person like me, that's exciting.
But not everyone is me. Some people just want to know the basics and learn as they go. That's not always easy in this industry.
Who I Am and Why I Wrote This Book

Writing on a wooden desk background. FocusWriter (Windows). View in high-resolution at www.authorlevelup.com/handbookimages.

Are customizable backgrounds a deal breaker for most authors? No. Most people don't care that much about it, but maybe you do, so that's why I included it in this book.

PRIVACY SETTINGS

For many writers, the act of writing is private. They don't like people even passing by in a coffee shop to see their words, let alone their family members read them. I'm definitely one of those writers; I don't like to let *anyone* see my work until it's ready to publish.

Did you know that there are writing apps on the market that offer privacy settings to help you keep your work private?

The first is password protection. Protect your projects with a password so no one accidentally stumbles upon your work if they happen to be using your computer.

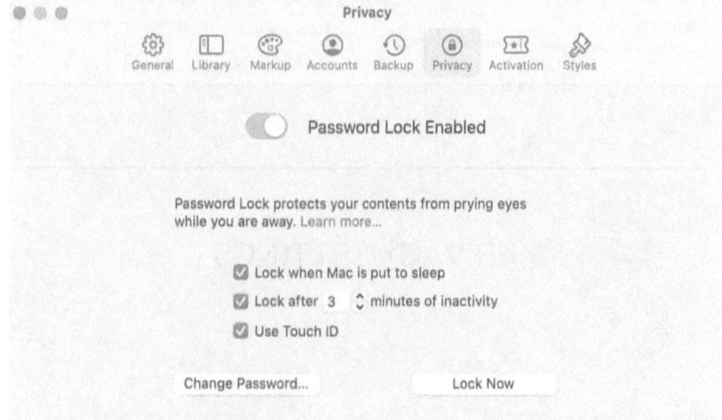

Password protection with Ulysses. (Mac). View in high-resolution at www.authorlevelup.com/handbookimages.

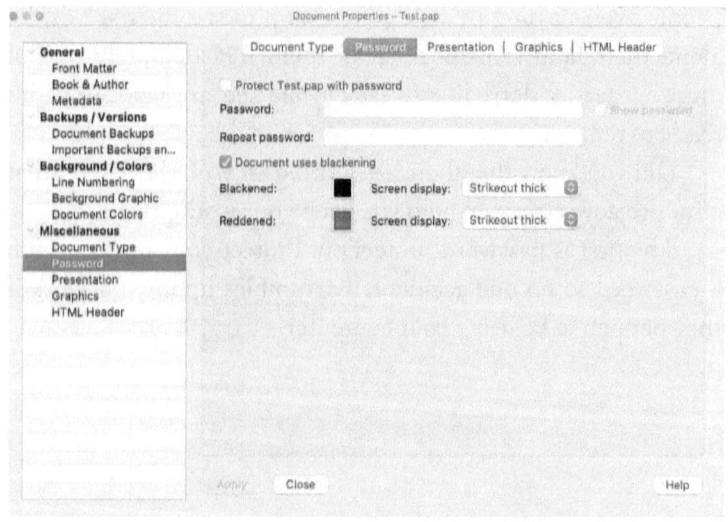

Password protection with Papyrus Author. The software also offers the ability to redact text. (Mac). View in high-resolution at www.authorlevelup.com/handbookimages.

This feature is a godsend for young writers who don't want

their parents to know what they're writing, or for writers who want to keep their work secret. However, be careful with password protection because if you forget your password, you're screwed.

Some apps also allow you to auto-quit a project after a certain time has passed, say 30 minutes. This feature is independent of password protection, and you're more likely to see it instead of passwords if an app only has one privacy feature.

As with all features, there's a time and a place for everything. I'd like to see more apps offer privacy settings. In the future.

OUTLINING AND RESEARCH

GENERAL OUTLINING TOOLS

They say that kitchens sell homes. If there's one feature that sells a writing app, it's outlining support.

Outlining is ultimately about being organized. Every author organizes their stories differently, sometimes differently with each novel. The best outlining features empower them to let their personalities shine.

I'll cover more specific outlining features in the next chapters, but first, there are some key factors we must consider.

Outlining Support or "Outlining Support"?

With a few notable exceptions, almost every writing app promises to help authors organize their stories. How they do that, however, is worth thinking about.

Some writing apps have true outlining features, including but not limited to:

- True outlines with nested hierarchies

- Timelines
- Corkboards or pin boards
- Index cards
- Synopses
- Plot grids

We'll discuss many of these features in the next sections. They help you arrange your story. They're often non-destructive, meaning that you can move them around and play with them to your heart's desire without hurting anything.

Some writing apps, however, don't have true outlining support. They may offer the ability to create a "plot" folder or page, but it's just a blank document that you have to fill out.

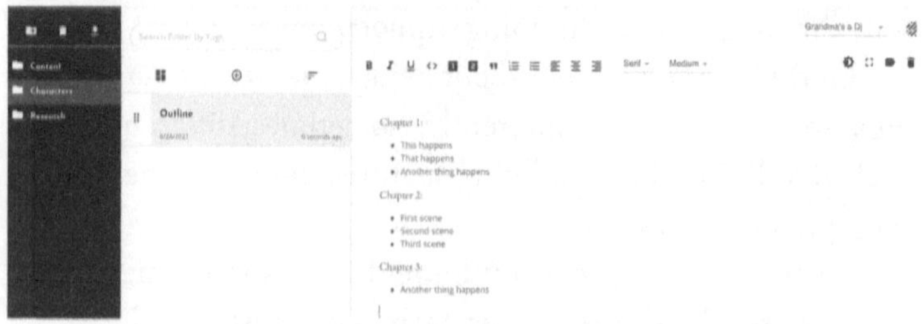

Simple outline document in Scrylis. Filling out this page is no different from writing a chapter. (Web-Based). View in high-resolution at www.authorlevelup.com/handbookimages.

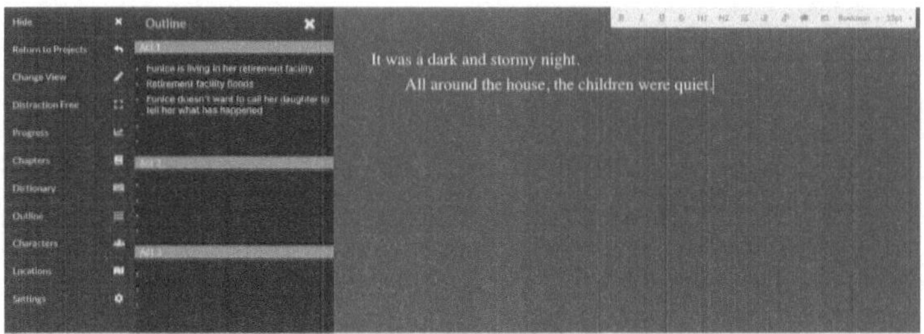

Outlining in Cetacean. The outline rests in the middle panel and is visible while you're writing the story. This is a simple outlining feature that offers the ability to create an outline hierarchy. (Web-Based). View in high-resolution at www. authorlevelup.com/handbookimages.

That's not a diss on developers, but let's be honest about what outlining is and what authors need. That said, some authors are fine with limited outlining support because they may not need sophisticated tools to help them outline, or they may not outline their books at all.

Writers can easily fall into what I call outlining hell—when they use amazing outlining features and never get around to writing their novel. This is why I don't view the lack of such a feature as a negative. There are pros and cons to both approaches, but the key is which type of feature works for you.

Also, it's worth noting that while many writing apps offer outlining support, you may find that a dedicated outlining app is better for your needs. Apps like Campfire and Plottr do a great job at helping you manage the "pre-production" of your story, and they offer the ability to export your data so that you can import it easily into your writing app (if your writing app supports importing media). If I were to buy outlining software, this import-export relationship would be the most important factor in my buying decision.

Overall, make sure you decide what type of outlining approach you need.

CORKBOARD

In the old days, writers outlined their stories by hand. Some would write scenes on index cards (or sticky notes), and they would scatter the index cards all over their desk (or kitchen table). Then, they'd pin the cards on a cork board or presentation board to serve as their guiding force while writing. The cork board was a helpful tool for outlining, free association of ideas, and organization.

This tradition is still alive today, and all you have to do is search for "outline a novel with index cards" to see how some authors use this approach.

Today, writing apps emulate the index and cork board by offering an endless virtual board with unlimited digital index cards or sticky notes.

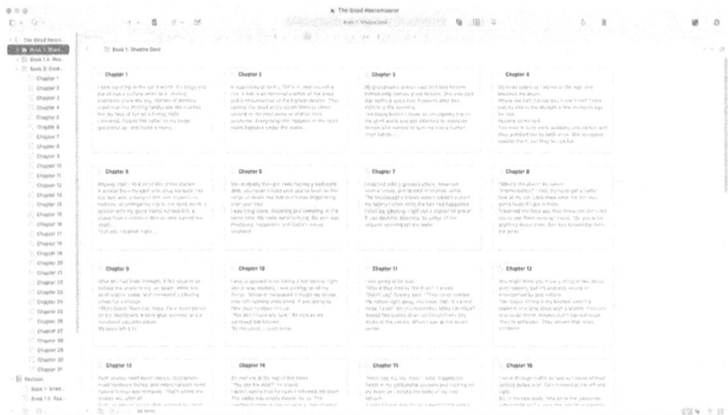

Scrivener's Corkboard gives you virtual index cards for each chapter. (Mac). View in high-resolution at www.authorlevelup. com/handbookimages.

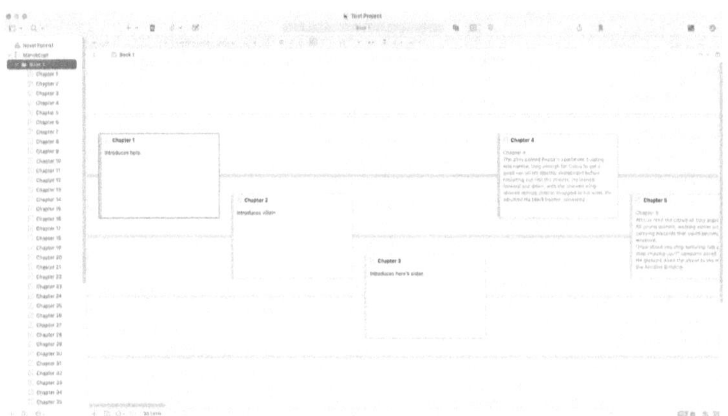

Scrivener's Threaded Corkboard allows you to create a pseudo-timeline. In this image, each color represents a character's POV. (Mac). View in high-resolution at www. authorlevelup.com/handbookimages.

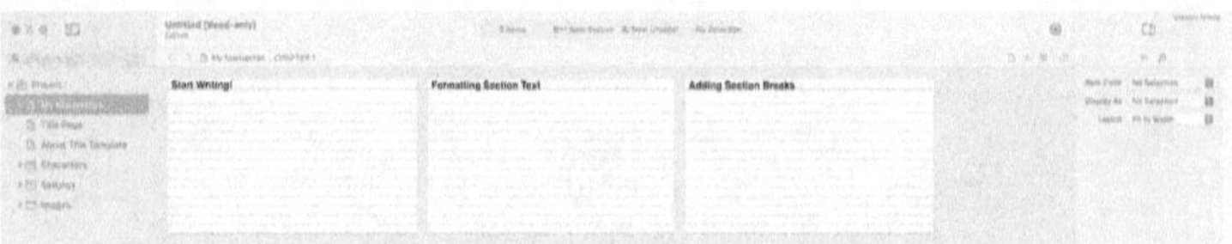

Storyist's Corkboard (Mac). View in high-resolution at www.authorlevelup.com/handbookimages.

Papyrus Author's Pinboard (Mac). View in high-resolution at
www.authorlevelup.com/handbookimages.

Cork boards have rich feature sets. They may include some
or all of the list below.

- Your chapters are represented on the cork board, and you can write synopses for them.
- You can write chapter synopses for index cards or notes.
- Non-impactful rearrangement; rearrange your cards and notes without fear of hurting your data.
- Impactful rearrangement; rearrange the order of your chapters in your manuscript whenever you move your cards.
- Threaded cork board; use your cork board as a timeline to track multiple characters.

You'll either use the cork board feature every day or not at all. When I started using Scrivener, I made sure my cork board always looked good. Now that I've written over 60 books, I don't pay much attention to the feature at all anymore.

Whether you prefer a cork board, pin board, or a wall of digital sticky notes, there is no doubt that this feature will help you get more organized, especially when you use it along with a split-screen, floating window, or dual monitor setup so you can have your story and outline open at the same time.

CHARACTER, SETTING, AND ITEM MANAGEMENT

Outlining is more than figuring out what happens in your story; it's also about discovering your characters, setting, and special items. Writing apps have features to help you manage these elements too.

Character management is the most prominent feature, but it's not uncommon to see setting management, and, to a lesser extent, item management.

The most common way this feature shows up is through a character profile, which allows you to build profiles of your characters. Typically, you can include profiles, biographies, and even upload pictures of actors who look like your characters.

This feature is diverse across apps, and every writing app approaches it differently. If this is an important feature for you, make sure to do your homework (and use the Writing App Database and filter by "Outlining Support" to get a list of apps that offer the feature).

To give you a sense of how different this feature can be across writing apps, let's take Storyist for Mac. It offers the ability to see your characters on a corkboard-like feature.

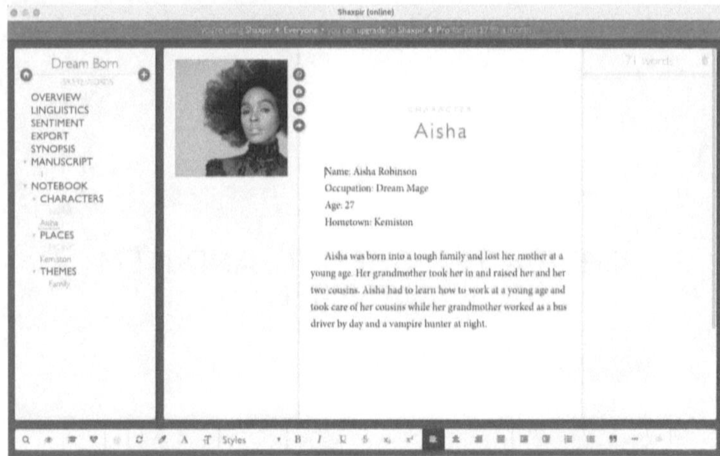

Shaxpir's character template sheet. (Mac). View in high-resolution at www.authorlevelup.com/handbookimages.

Storyist has a page template called a character sheet, which comes with pre-filled questions that you can add, edit, and delete based on your preferences. Scrivener also offers a similar page template for settings.

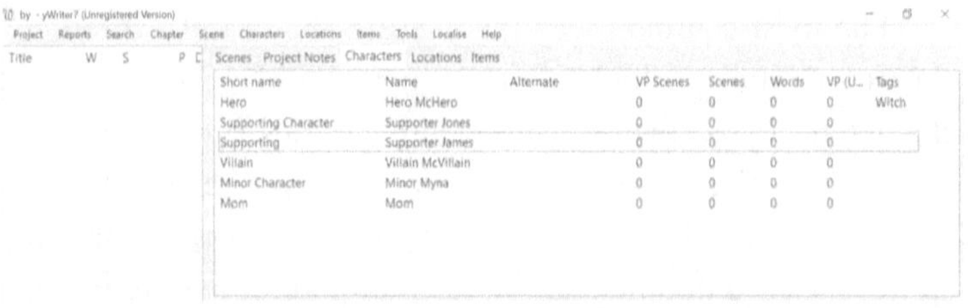

yWriter allows you to create a character database. (Windows). View in high-resolution at www.authorlevelup. com/handbookimages.

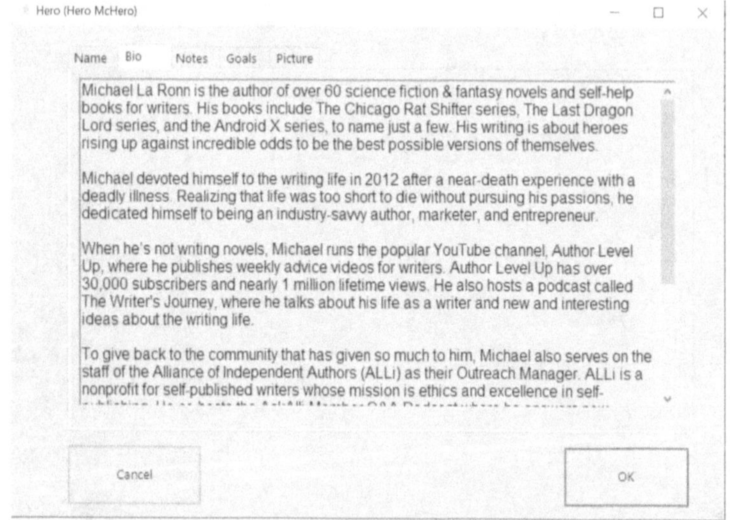

yWriter character database detail. (Windows). View in high-resolution at www.authorlevelup.com/handbookimages.

Scrivener also offers advanced chapter tagging and meta-data management to help you keep characters straight and when they appear in the story.

Title and Synopsis	Label	Status	Section Type	Words
Chapter 1 Introduces hero.	Cyrus	No Status	Scene	1,250
Chapter 2 Introduces villain	Thurst...	No Status	Scene	3,158
Chapter 3 Introduces hero's sister.	Becca	No Status	Scene	1,285
Chapter 4	Cyrus	No Status	Scene	2,287
Chapter 5	Thurst...	No Status	Scene	1,686
Chapter 6	Cyrus	No Status	Scene	2,751
Chapter 7	Thurst...	No Status	Scene	1,309
Chapter 8	Cyrus	No Status	Scene	1,112
Chapter 9	No Label	No Status	Scene	2,221
Chapter 10	No Label	No Status	Scene	1,446
Chapter 11	No Label	No Status	Scene	1,122
Chapter 12	No Label	No Status	Scene	2,680
Chapter 13	No Label	No Status	Scene	815
Chapter 14	No Label	No Status	Scene	867
Chapter 15	No Label	No Status	Scene	1,227
Chapter 16	No Label	No Status	Scene	852
Chapter 17	No Label	No Status	Scene	273
Chapter 18	No Label	No Status	Scene	2,582
Chapter 19	No Label	No Status	Scene	998
Chapter 20	No Label	No Status	Scene	275
Chapter 21	No Label	No Status	Scene	466
Chapter 22	No Label	No Status	Scene	1,898
Chapter 23	No Label	No Status	Scene	1,303
Chapter 24	No Label	No Status	Scene	2,947
Chapter 25	No Label	No Status	Scene	1,965
Chapter 26	No Label	No Status	Scene	574
Chapter 27	No Label	No Status	Scene	1,583
Chapter 28	No Label	No Status	Scene	1,406

Scrivener's outline mode. (Mac). View in high-resolution at www.authorlevelup.com/handbookimages.

And Living Writer, which has the most interesting take on this feature, offers the ability to "tag" your characters so that you can keep track of which chapters they appear in. This is amazingly innovative and helpful for people who follow the "Writing into the Dark" method.

Living Writer's Story Element feature. You can see it at work in the bottom left. When you type, it will prompt you to tag each character. You will then see the character name highlighted. (Web-Based). View in high-resolution at www. authorlevelup.com/handbookimages.

As you can see, you have a lot of choices, and I barely covered them in this chapter.

You can store your character work in your binder so it's always available to you when you're writing.

It's worth noting that if this is an important feature to you, then it's best to choose a WYSIWYG writing app. I've yet to see a Markdown app accomplish character management. It's just not suited for the Markdown environment.

TIMELINES

Timelines are unique features and users need very specific things with them. You may require such a feature in your writing app, and, if you do, only a handful of writing apps offer the ability to create a true timeline. You may be better served using a dedicated timeline app like Aeon Timeline. Other people like good ol' Microsoft Excel.

That said, timelining does show up in writing apps occasionally.

Write It Now offers this feature.

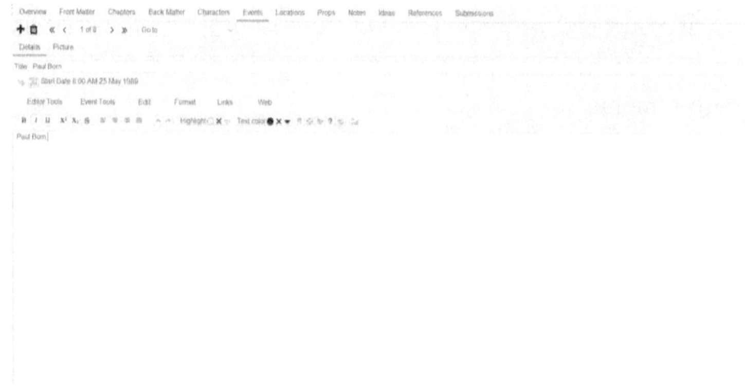

Write It Now 6's timeline functionality in action. (Windows).
View in high-resolution at www.authorlevelup.com/
handbookimages.

Scrivener's threaded cork board can also serve as a timeline, though timeline purists would probably need something more robust.

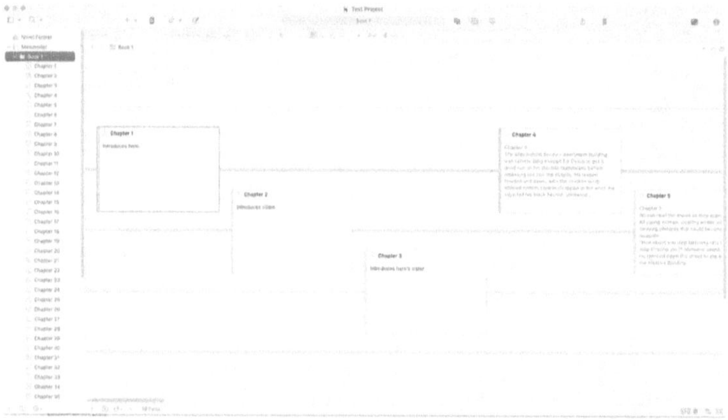

Scrivener's Threaded Corkboard is a great feature but may not meet true timeline needs. (Mac). View in high-resolution at www.authorlevelup.com/handbookimages.

If you need a timeline, make sure to evaluate it based on your needs, and use the app's trial period to see if meets your requirements.

FEATURES FOR GETTING RESEARCH
INTO YOUR NOVEL

Every writer has to do research at some point. The question is how research can be brought into the app.

Research takes many forms, and you can't control what format your sources will be in. If you encounter an interesting place on a map, you should be able to save a picture of the map into your writing app's binder. If you encounter a public domain record, you should be able to import a PDF of that too. If you find a short audio clip of a chant that you want to integrate into your story, you also want to be able to preserve that so you can return to it later.

Some writers may prefer to use a note-taking app like Evernote or OneNote for convenience. Those apps are easier to do research in because you can use their web clippers to get content off the internet quickly.

That said, Papyrus Author offers a drag-and-drop feature that lets you drag content from the internet into the app. It also lets you create a research database.

If importing research is important to you, then I recommend choosing a writing app that supports importing a wide variety of media. Formats include but are not limited to:

- Microsoft Word .DOC/DOCX
- PDF
- HTML
- Images
- MP3/Video (or at least a way to link to them)

Just be aware that if you store too much content within your writing app, it may take longer to load your files and the app performance can suffer.

The goal should be for your research to "live" in your writing app alongside your story. The key is finding a writing app that makes this as easy as possible.

ORGANIZATION

How do you organize your writing? The topic of organization is deeply personal; some writers couldn't care less about organizing their projects, but other writers are organizational task masters. For the latter group, everything has to be a certain way.

Whether you want a loose or rigid structure for organizing your project, the features in this section will help you make up your mind.

Don't underestimate the importance of being organized in your writing app. Even if you don't organize your project until the end, you'll still need to refer to it later. It's amazing how often you need to open your old projects for one reason or another.

"SMART" DOC/DOCX IMPORTING AND CHAPTER SPLITTING

When I do writing app demos, people are usually impressed with the writing app. I like to show people how to set up their books in the app, but the most common use-case is when a writer wants to switch to that app and wants to bring in an existing manuscript. A "smart" import feature makes this easier.

Depending on the writing app you choose, you'll spend a few seconds or a few hours importing existing manuscripts. This feature is that important.

Many apps allow you to import a Microsoft Word document, which is how most writers will have existing manuscripts saved. That's rarely an issue, as many writing apps must have Word document support to some degree.

The problem is with your chapter breaks. Will the app break up your chapter properly, or will YOU have to do it? Will the app recognize bulleted lists, hyperlinks, heading styles, and so on?

It sounds trivial, but trust me when I say that spending an entire afternoon cleaning up your manuscript after an import is not fun. I would suggest that you avoid it if possible. If you're a prolific writer wanting to switch writing apps and your new app doesn't have this feature, you should email the developer and demand it. Technical issues aside, this is one of the few writing app features that is unacceptable not to have.

To have a clean import, your file must be clean, which means that you will have to use conventional (and typically Microsoft Word) formatting best practices, which primarily includes using proper section breaks and header styles in your document *before* you import it into the writing app. This is a downside if you aren't already doing this, but it will make your life easier.

If you take the time to prepare your document correctly, you will benefit from a feature called "smart import" if your writing app supports it. With a "smart" import, your writing app reads your document and then formats it as closely as possible to the original. This means splitting up your chapter, honoring your existing formatting (within reason), and so on.

Scrivener offers an "import file and split" feature that allows you to split your chapters based on conventional section breaks and headers or by a special symbol.

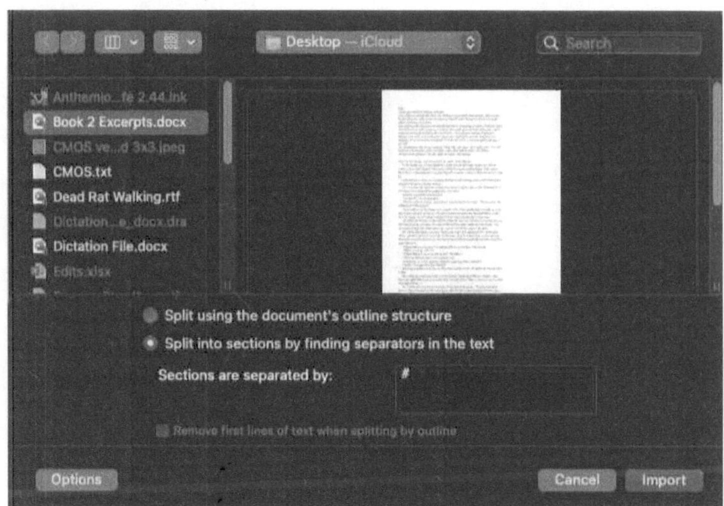

Scrivener's import and split feature allows for quick and easy import of manuscripts into the program. (Mac). View in high-resolution at www.authorlevelup.com/handbookimages.

When you avail yourself of these features, you can bring your manuscript into your new writing app of choice in seconds and start writing almost immediately. You'll save hours of frustration.

Another similar feature (but not identical) to smart importing is chapter splitting. A chapter split feature allows you to split all text after the cursor into a separate chapter. This is also an acceptable way to import existing manuscripts, though it is more work.

If you can, take advantage of this kind of assistance to ensure you don't spend hours fixing your manuscript after import.

SEARCH

You'd be amazed at how often you need to search for something in your book. You may need to find and fix inconsistencies in your book, such as character names, or you may need to simply find a passage you want to reference.

Most writing apps offer basic search, but not all offer *robust* search.

I like to think of search functionality in terms of levels.

Level 1: Basic search. You can find and replace words and phrases.

Level 2: Advanced search. You can find and replace words, but also search by formatting, such as bold, links, and so on.

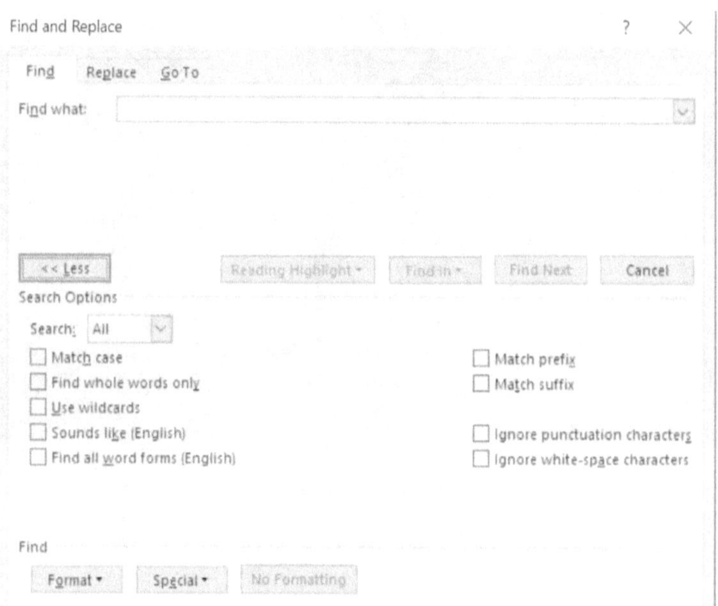

Microsoft Word's Advanced Find allows you to search by formatting and other special criteria. (Windows). View in high-resolution at www.authorlevelup.com/handbookimages.

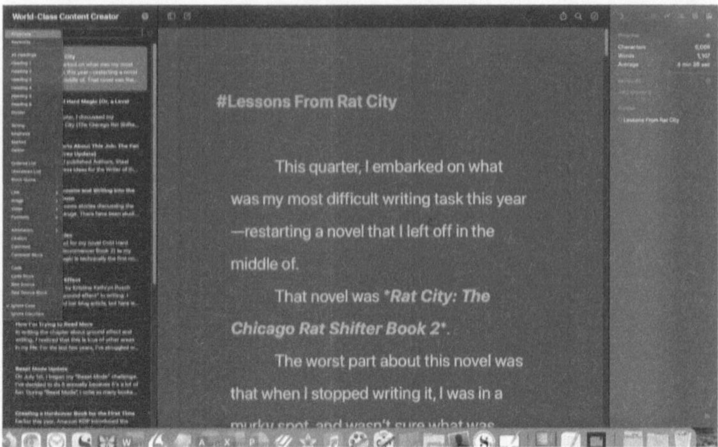

Ulysses allows you to search by each different Markdown element. The search bar is a dropdown on the left-hand side of the screen. (Mac). View in high-resolution at www. authorlevelup.com/handbookimages.

Level 3: Intermediate search. You can find and replace words and phrases, but you can also see how often they appear at the project level, usually with a visual guide.

Microsoft Word's search bar feature. The highlighted chapters are where the word can be found. (Windows). View in high-resolution at www.authorlevelup.com/handbookimages.

Level 4: Universal search. This search allows you to search across everything you've ever written. This type of search is exclusive to apps with universal libraries.

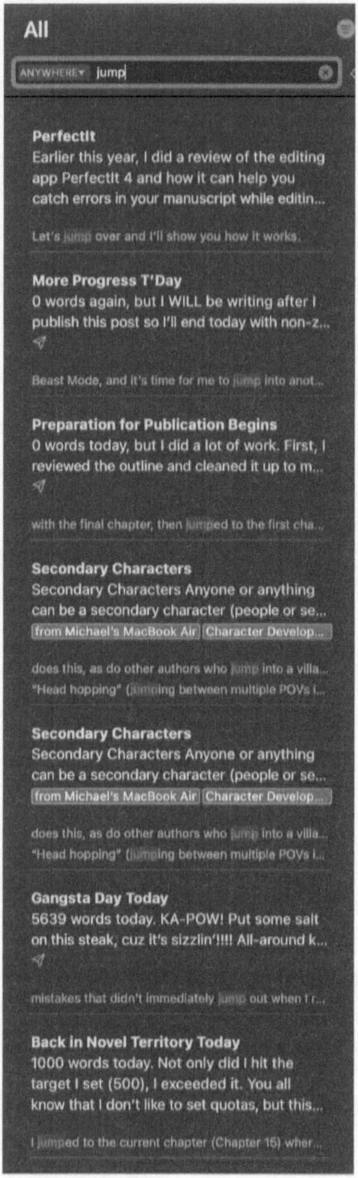

All

ANYWHERE▾ jump

PerfectIt
Earlier this year, I did a review of the editing app PerfectIt 4 and how it can help you catch errors in your manuscript while editin...

Let's jump over and I'll show you how it works.

More Progress T'Day
0 words again, but I WILL be writing after I publish this post so I'll end today with non-z...

Beast Mode, and it's time for me to jump into anot...

Preparation for Publication Begins
0 words today, but I did a lot of work. First, I reviewed the outline and cleaned it up to m...

with the final chapter, then jumped to the first cha...

Secondary Characters
Secondary Characters Anyone or anything can be a secondary character (people or se...
from Michael's MacBook Air   Character Develop...

does this, as do other authors who jump into a villa...
"Head hopping" (jumping between multiple POVs i...

Secondary Characters
Secondary Characters Anyone or anything can be a secondary character (people or se...
from Michael's MacBook Air   Character Develop...

does this, as do other authors who jump into a villa...
"Head hopping" (jumping between multiple POVs i...

Gangsta Day Today
5639 words today. KA-POW! Put some salt on this steak, cuz it's sizzlin'!!!! All-around k...

mistakes that didn't immediately jump out when I r...

Back in Novel Territory Today
1000 words today. Not only did I hit the target I set (500), I exceeded it. You all know that I don't like to set quotas, but this...

I jumped to the current chapter (Chapter 15) wher...

Ulysses's universal library. The results are every instance of the word "jump" across an entire library of manuscripts—not just one. (Mac). View in high-resolution at www.authorlevelup. com/handbookimages.

If this is an important feature for you, I wouldn't recommend anything less than Level 3.

THE WRITING EXPERIENCE

Now we come to the most important part of any writing app: the writing experience. An app can have every feature imaginable, but if it doesn't feel good when you're writing, it won't matter.

First, we must discuss the word processor. How does it feel when you are typing your words? Good? Awkward? For example, desktop writing apps often have a pleasant keyboard-to-eye feel. When you press a button on your keyboard, the button depresses smoothly, and a letter shows up on your screen in a manner so fluidly, you probably never thought about it until now. I call this "typing umami," and I've become keenly aware of it after testing dozens and dozens of writing apps. I can't describe it eloquently, but I know it when I feel it. And I especially know when it's not there. Hopefully, you will too.

If you write on your phone, the tactile sensation of typing on a glass screen is much different. Not every app has "typing umami." Only a few do. I find that some mobile writing app keyboards feel stunted, and there is a slight lag between touching the key and the letter appearing on the screen. It took me a while to find the right mobile writing app that felt good in my hands.

The same is true when you write in the browser. The sensation of writing in a browser is different from writing in a writing app, even though you're using the same keyboard. Pay attention to the next time you're typing in a URL in your browser versus your next chapter in your preferred writing app. There's a difference.

You want to find the "typing umami" in any app that you use, whether it be on a desktop, phone, or browser. You're going to spend the majority of your time writing, so it should be comfortable. If not, you'll find that the very task of typing will be more tedious than it should be. This may subconsciously lead you to *not* use the writing app as much as you want to.

You'll know what "typing umami" feels like when you find your perfect writing app because when you switch to write in another app, it won't feel the same. It's like your last car; that car was so comfortable and worn in that it probably took you quite some time to get used to your new car.

Second, we discussed toolbars earlier. That's another important part of the writing experience. Every feature you need should be a click or keyboard shortcut away. Every writing app has a learning curve, but even if after several months, you still feel like you're fishing for features, you probably haven't found your perfect match. The best writing apps (for you) should fit you like a glove. It should become an extension of your fingers that help you write faster and smarter and in less time. Keep that in mind as we review the features in this section.

TEXT ZOOMING

Everyone's eyesight is different, and the ability to zoom in and out of your text is a godsend. Most writing apps support text zooming, but I included it as a key feature in this book because some don't, at least not in their infancy.

Desktop and mobile writing apps almost always have zooming, but browser-based writing apps often lack it. I suspect that this is a browser limitation. I haven't found a web-based writing app yet that supports zooming, though some do have it on their roadmap at the time of this writing.

You can use your browser's zoom feature, but that zooms the entire window in and out, which is not desirable when you're done writing and just want to browse the internet. However, that's the best workaround at this time.

I've shown browser-based apps to writers, and people get excited about them, only to realize that there's no zoom functionality. It's a buzzkill, especially for those writers who love the apps but not the lack of zooming!

I don't have the greatest eyesight in the world, so text zooming is an essential feature for me. It's one of those features you don't think about too much but desperately wish for it when it's absent.

TYPEWRITER MODE

I'm old enough to remember what it was like to write on a typewriter. My dad had an old typewriter that he used at his job. His boss replaced the typewriter with the computer, and because his boss had no need for old technology, he sent my dad home with it.

Occasionally, I'd tell my dad I wanted to write. He'd go to the closet, lug out the dull green typewriter, and load paper into it.

Talk about "typing umami"! There is no comparison to how a typewriter feels under your fingers. Not one.

The springy metal keys under your fingertips, the clickety-clack noises they make, the hammers beating the page with ink, the warmth of the paper in your hands, fresh out of the machine. I have fond memories of writing stories on that (not so) little typewriter.

With such a memorable writing experience, it's no surprise that many thirst for the old typewriter feel. Fortunately, there's a writing app for that!

Enter typewriter mode, a digital simulation of writing on a typewriter.

Normally, when you write in a word processor and press the Enter key, the cursor jumps to the next line. If you want to scroll down, you must use your mouse or the little elevator on the side of the writing app. In typewriter mode, when you hit the Return key, your text is pushed upward, just like in a typewriter. The only thing missing is the key noise.

Typewriter mode is often combined with a full-screen or distraction-free mode for the best results. This way, the only thing on the screen is your text.

Typewriter mode is usually an option that you can turn on and off. It is not the writing app's main mode of operation.

This is a great feature if you have nostalgia for the old ways.

WRITING IN MULTIPLE TABS
AND/OR WINDOWS

It's universally accepted that working on dual monitors makes you more productive. This is why employers across the world provide dual monitors to their employees.

If that's true for general computing, then it's probably true for writing apps too. If you have your outline in a separate window while you write your story, you don't have to waste clicks to bring it up whenever you need to consult it. If you're editing, it helps to have a few windows open sometimes, especially if you need to cross-reference chapters.

There are many ways to accomplish this productivity boost.

The first is through a split-screen feature. This allows you to have two windows side-by-side or on top of one another so that you can work more efficiently.

Scrivener also has a robust split-screen feature that lets you orient the windows vertically or horizontally.

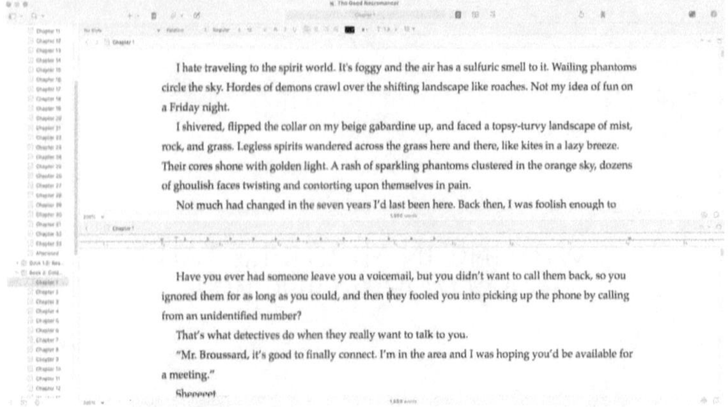

Scrivener's split-screen feature. The top screen is Chapter 1 of Book 1 of a series, and the bottom is Chapter 1 of Book 2. (Mac). View in high-resolution at www.authorlevelup.com/handbookimages.

Scrivener even supports up to four split screens at the same time!

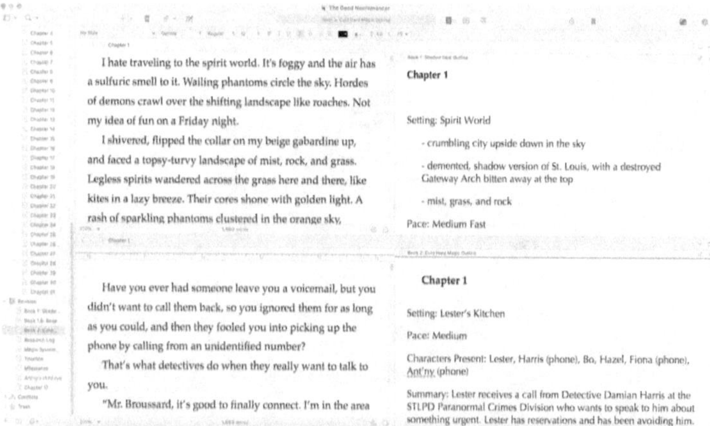

Scrivener's copyholder feature lets you create up to four split screens at the same time. In this example, the top screens contain Chapters 1 and 2 of a Book 1 and the bottom screens contain Chapters 1 and 2 of a Book 2. (Mac). View in high-resolution at www.authorlevelup.com/handbookimages.

The second way to accomplish multiple windows is through multiple tabs. This works exactly how your browser works.

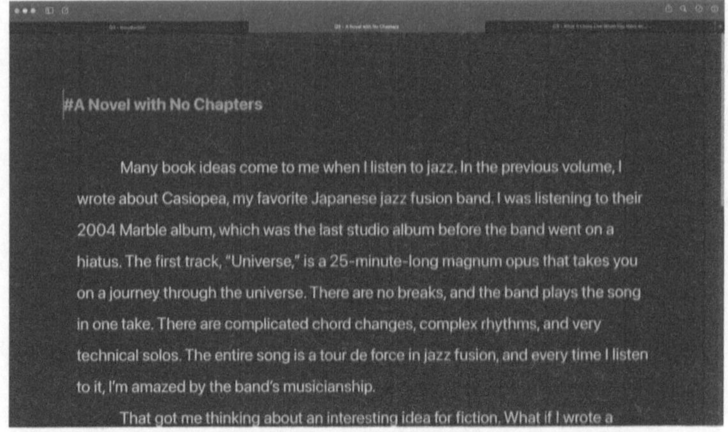

Ulysses's tab feature. Each tab represents a chapter in the book. (Mac). View in high-resolution at www.authorlevelup. com/handbookimages.

The third way to accomplish multiple windows is through multiple window support. Ulysses perhaps has the best multiple window feature of any writing app I've ever used. You can have an infinite number of windows open, and each one functions as its own version of Ulysses. The app even has tab support, so each of your windows can have tabs too.

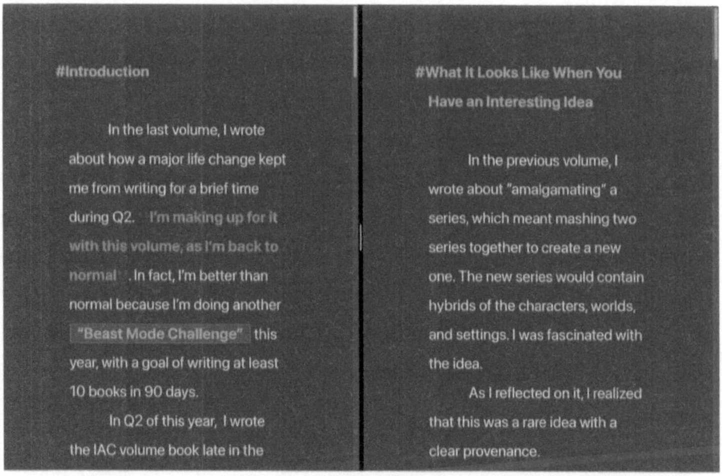

#Introduction

In the last volume, I wrote about how a major life change kept me from writing for a brief time during Q2. I'm making up for it with this volume, as I'm back to normal. In fact, I'm better than normal because I'm doing another "Beast Mode Challenge" this year, with a goal of writing at least 10 books in 90 days.

In Q2 of this year, I wrote the IAC volume book late in the

#What It Looks Like When You Have an Interesting Idea

In the previous volume, I wrote about "amalgamating" a series, which meant mashing two series together to create a new one. The new series would contain hybrids of the characters, worlds, and settings. I was fascinated with the idea.

As I reflected on it, I realized that this was a rare idea with a clear provenance.

My primary monitor with two Ulysses windows side-by-side using the Mac snap assist feature. (Mac). View in high-resolution at www.authorlevelup.com/handbookimages.

#A Novel with No Chapters

Many book ideas come to me when I listen to jazz. In the previous volume, I wrote about Casiopea, my favorite Japanese jazz fusion band. I was listening to their 2004 Marble album, which was the last studio album before the band went on a hiatus. The first track, "Universe," is a 25-minute-long magnum opus that takes you on a journey through the universe. There are no breaks, and the band plays the song in one take. There are complicated chord changes, complex rhythms, and very technical solos. The entire song is a tour de force in jazz fusion, and every time I listen to it, I'm amazed by the band's musicianship.

That got me thinking about an interesting idea for fiction. What if I wrote a

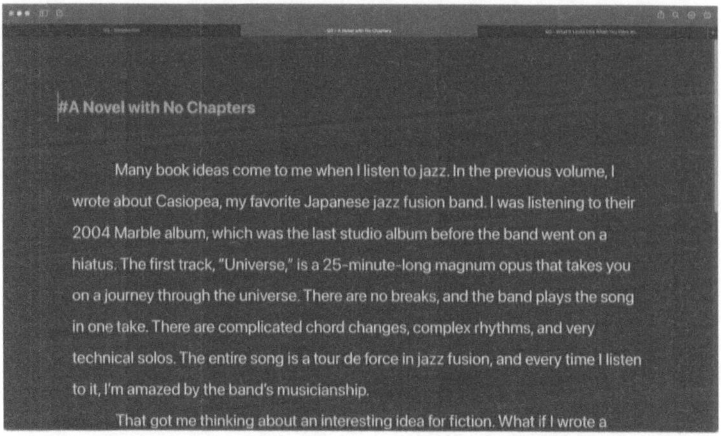

My second monitor with a Ulysses window with tabs. (Mac). View in high-resolution at www.authorlevelup.com/handbookimages.

In a web-based browser, you can accomplish the same

purpose by having two different tabs or windows of the same project open at the same time, if your app supports that.

The good news is that you have many options.

Even though multiple windows and tabs can boost productivity, you can go overboard. There is such a thing as having *too many* tabs or windows open. Just because you can have fifteen windows open doesn't mean you should. That said, this is an amazingly helpful feature that will help you write books faster and more efficiently, especially if you pair it with keyboard shortcuts and/or dual monitors.

PAGE VIEW

Some authors prefer to work within the visual confines of a page. For these authors, the endless scroll of a white or black background disorients them. Page view gives you a structure, and when your words reach the end of that page, the app creates a new page.

Given that most people's first encounter with a writing app is in a page format, it's not a surprise that some people prefer this feature because it's familiar.

Fortunately, every WYSIWYG writing app that I know of supports page view and I don't need to show you images of it.

You won't find page modes in Markdown apps because that's against the philosophy of Markdown.

Because Markdown controls how your book looks *after* you export, it doesn't support page breaks, because if you think about it, Markdown is for digital formats and digital devices have different screen sizes. If page view is important to you, you may want to steer away from Markdown apps.

WORD COUNT TRACKING AND STATISTICS

I always like to know where my book's word count sits. Almost every writing app I tested shows you your word count at the chapter level and the project level.

Almost all writing apps also offer text statistics that show you the number of words, characters, lines, and so on in your project.

However, there's more power hidden in your word counts.

First, there's the ability to track your word counts over time, like in Scrivener's Writing History feature:

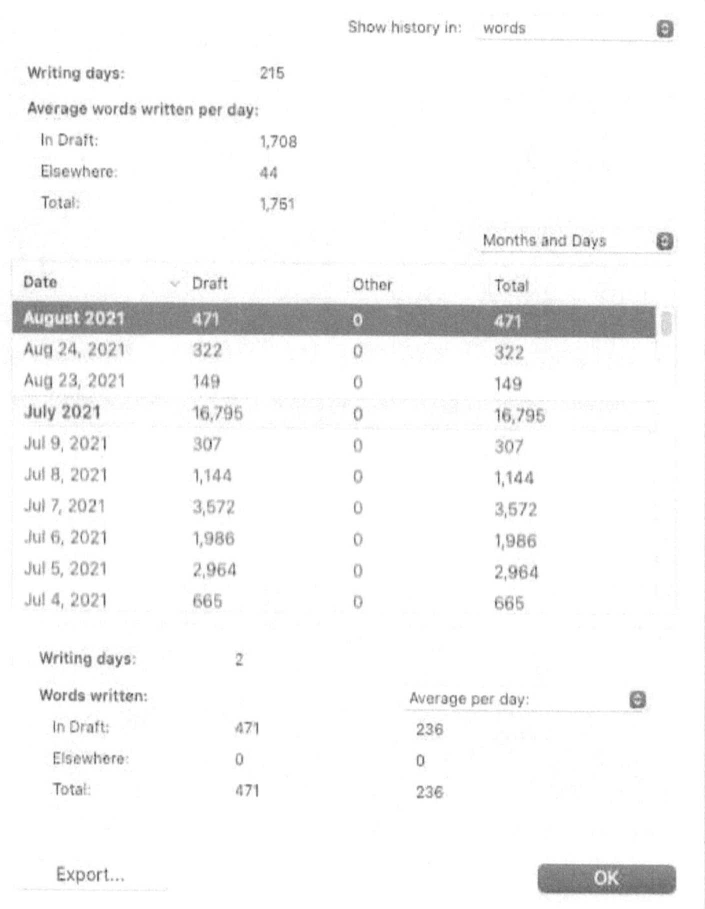

Scrivener's Writing History feature. (Mac). View in high-resolution at www.authorlevelup.com/handbookimages.

Tracking your word counts over time is great because it gives you a realistic look at how you're writing versus what you think you're doing.

Some apps also let you see a status bar that shows you how well you're doing against your goals.

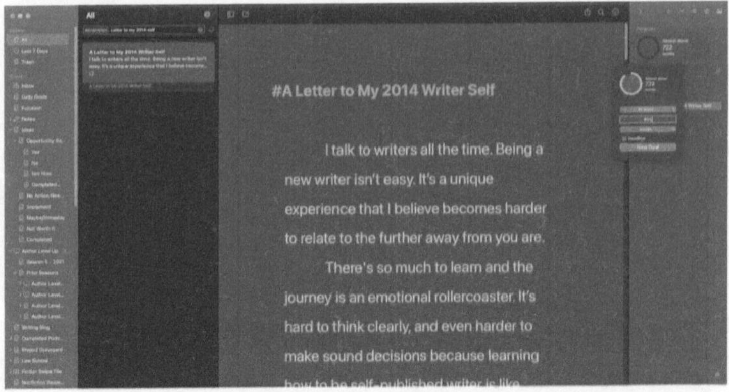

Ulysses's status circle. You can see it on the right-hand side of the screen. (Mac). View in high-resolution at www.authorlevelup.com/handbookimages.

Second, there's the ability to set deadlines and targets for your word counts, like what Dabble Writer offers:

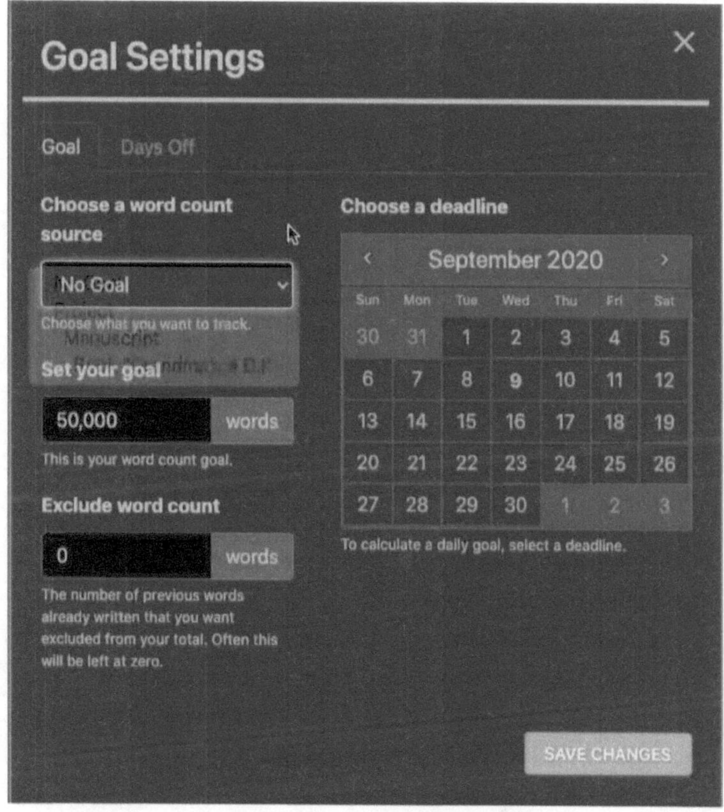

Dabble's word count and goal tracker. (Web-Based). View in high-resolution at www.authorlevelup.com/handbookimages.

I find the writing history and word count features very useful in my daily writing activities. I always want to know how many words I have written for the day, and how many I wrote for the month. These features will keep you in the know.

COMMENTS AND TRACKED
CHANGES

Until very recently, I used to think *true* tracked changes in a writing app was a white whale that was unreasonable to ask for outside of Microsoft Word.

Microsoft Word is the gold standard of tracked changes. It's the primary reason why writers need to export to Microsoft Word because that's the tool editors use to provide edits. Google Docs also has pretty good tracked changes functionality too.

Along with paperback formatting, tracked changes are one of the great pain points of the writing process. No features are more important to solve if we want to see writing apps of the future.

If it weren't for tracked changes, you could keep your entire manuscript in the same ecosystem if you wanted, assuming you chose a writing app that offered full-featured e-book and paperback formatting. You could simply export your book to Word format, send it to your editor, and when you received your edits, you could reimport the Word file with tracked changes. Then, all you'd have to do is accept the changes and export your book for publication. Tracked changes are that big of a deal.

Yet, in app after app that I tested, I didn't see tracked

changes anywhere. I thought maybe the feature was so difficult that it wasn't worth programming.

And then, I stumbled upon Papyrus Author. Not does it support tracked changes, it supports them fully. You can import a Word document from your editor and you can work on your tracked changes within Papyrus Author.

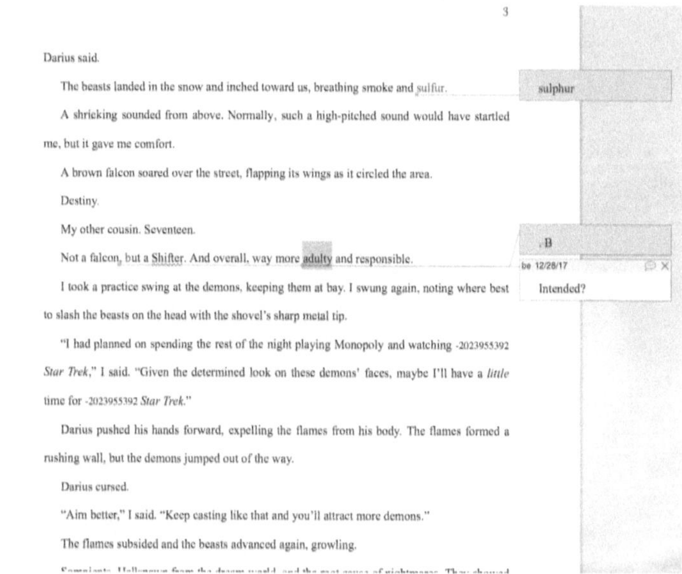

Tracked changes with Papyrus Author. It works identical to the same feature in Microsoft Word and Google Docs. The text in this image was imported from the Word document my editor sent me. (Mac). View in high-resolution at www.authorlevelup.com/handbookimages.

If the developers of Papyrus Author can do it, we should demand this from other writing apps too.

THE FORMATTING EXPERIENCE

Formatting is where writing apps diverge. Some writing apps offer very little formatting ability; others can format e-books but not paperbacks; others can format e-books *and* paperbacks but paperback formatting is limited; a rare few can do it all.

Whether formatting is important to you or not, you need to make a major decision. You need to decide:

- if you want to format e-books and paperbacks within your writing app; or
- if you want to format e-books and paperbacks in a separate, dedicated formatting app (such as Adobe InDesign, Vellum, or Atticus); or
- if you want to hire a formatter.

If you want to do your formatting within the writing app, you automatically limit your options to just a few choices. If you choose to format your books outside of your writing app, then you have more flexibility and can use any writing app.

As we move into formatting, keep in mind that e-book and paperback formatting are two distinct features. While they share commonalities, you need to evaluate every writing app based on how well (and easily) they do *both*.

THE MOST IMPORTANT FORMATS TO EXPORT

Let's talk about the most important formats that a writing app needs to export. We'll break the list into must-haves and nice-to-haves.

Must-Have Export Formats

Microsoft Word .DOCX. You need a Word file to work with your editor. If an app can't produce this, you'll have to go through an extra step to create one. You also need a Word document if you wish to submit to many literary magazines.

Electronic Publication (ePUB). This is the universal e-book format accepted by e-book retailers. Not only must a writing app export to ePUB, but it also must create ePUBs that pass ePUB validation; otherwise, retailers won't accept your book.

Portable Digital Format (PDF). PDF is how paperback editions must be uploaded. Paperback PDFs must follow strict guidelines; just exporting your book to PDF format is not enough. Plus, some readers like to read PDFs on their computers. You can think of the PDF export as two different files: one as a paperback export and the other as a convenience for readers who don't have or like to read on dedicated reading devices. Both have different technical requirements.

If a writing app cannot export DOCX, ePUB, *and* print-ready PDFs, then it does not offer full formatting functionality.

Nice-to-Have Formats

Rich Text File (.RTF). This is a flexible text file format. It's not necessary for publication, but nice to keep an additional format of your book on file in case your other formats are corrupted.

Hypertext Markup Language (HTML). HTML is useful if you ever want to publish your work on your website, or if you use your writing app to write blog posts.

Again, these formats are nice to have, but not required.

E-BOOK FORMATTING

What is an e-book? It's a digital version of a book that is consumed in a browser, e-reader, or mobile devices such as a smartphone or tablet.

An e-book is a glorified HTML file. Each chapter in an e-book is a sequence of HTML code, with a wrapper that tells a device how to display it.

Take a look at the same text in a file ready for production and the actual source code that your device reads.

I

Ancestral Bogs, Western Continent
Year 1020

The wind whistled around his wings and the stars glittered off his black scales as Dark flapped furiously, pushing a torrent of air toward the ground to cushion him as he touched down on a rickety boardwalk in the middle of his family's ancestral bog. The boards trembled beneath his weight.

His claws scratched the rotting wood as he stood upright on all fours. The water, like purple velvet wavering in the starlight, seemed to swell upon his presence, sending slow, pulsing ripples downstream. He had prayed just yesterday at the altar of the bone-white mausoleum submerged in brush and shadow in the distance, offering a bloody tribute of heart and lungs to his grandfather in the great beyond, never imagining that it would be the starting point of a hunt today.

Dark folded his wings close to his body until they rubbed against his scales. He reached his long neck down and rubbed his nose against the wood.

He sniffed, taking in the remnants of peat long burned away, decaying fish, flecks of mercury on the water, and the blood and sweat of human slaves one hundred years ago toiling over this bridge. How they had screamed when Dark had struck them down. How they had gasped as the water pulled them under quickly and silently as Dark knelt and prayed.

Intermingled with it all, he sensed something fresh.

Sweat. Gathering in an armpit, pooling on the chest.

Yes, this sweat was recent.

An example of an e-book in Apple Books. (Mac). View in high-resolution at www.authorlevelup.com/handbookimages.

An example of the same chapter in HTML in Calibre. (Mac).
View in high-resolution at www.authorlevelup.com/
handbookimages.

I believe that every properly formatted e-book (and paperback) has two essential elements: utility and ease of navigation.

Readers want to read a book without the formatting getting in the way. They also need a good table of contents to help them navigate the book as needed.

That's it.

How do we obtain utility and ease of navigation? The answer depends on the format.

Let's start with e-books, and we'll return to utility and ease of navigation again when we discuss paperback formatting.

E-books are reflowable, which means that the text conforms to whatever device it is displayed on. Readers can also change the text size, font, and sizing between paragraphs.

Anything that artificially stops an e-book's reflowability is an enemy. Tabs are a prime example—they cause all sorts of problems in an e-book. The goal with an e-book is to format the text so that it appears well on any device.

Ease of navigation with e-books is all about the table of contents. An e-book has two types of tables of contents: a table of contents page that contains links to each chapter, and an NCX, which stands for Navigational Control XML, which allows the reader to jump between chapters on the fly no matter where they are in the book.

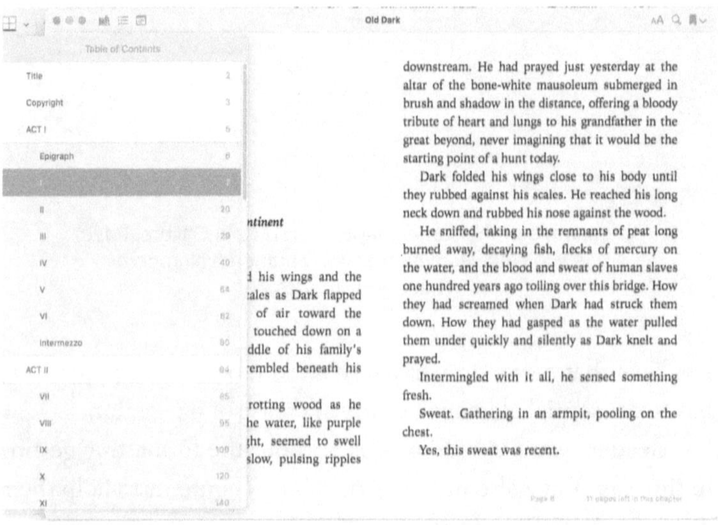

An NCX in action, which allows the reader to jump anywhere in the book. The NCX is on the left-hand side of the screen. View in high-resolution at www.authorlevelup.com/handbookimages.

That's as far as I can go into this topic without boring or frustrating you—learning the art of formatting is best taught visually.

Whether you are reading an e-book or a paperback, the best formatting is invisible and doesn't draw attention to itself.

Device Consistency

No reading device is the same, and if you try to format an e-book to look identical on every device, you'll give up. However, your book should look similar on different devices. While this isn't something you can always test in an app's trial mode, it's worth talking to other authors to learn what their experiences with the app have been.

With a dedicated formatting app, you have more features at your disposal, and you can always rest assured that they will render consistently across devices. While you may not have the same feature set with your writing app, you *do* want consistency across devices.

I bring this up because I tested a writing app where this went horribly wrong (I won't share the name because it was in beta when the error happened and the app is now defunct). The developer had a hell of a time trying to figure it out, and I'm not so sure that they ever solved it.

Always test your book formats on different devices—the worst thing that can happen is a reader emailing you telling you that your book on X retailer looks awful and you have no idea how to fix it because something is off with how your writing app generates an ePUB for that retailer. You've been warned.

Bells and Whistles

· · ·

The following items are not necessary to create a functional e-book, but they're nice to have if the app can do it.

Drop caps. These are large capital letters at the beginning of a chapter or section that occupies two lines.

Custom header images. These images appear at the top of a chapter. They can be flourishes, embellishments, or even include the chapter number.

Images. Images are anathema to e-books. They have to be sized correctly and formatted just right or they won't look good for readers. Plus, they balloon the book's file size, which will cost you in delivery fees on Amazon.

Those are the major bells and whistles. There are more, so do your homework.

PAPERBACK FORMATTING

Paperback formatting isn't fun unless you have a dedicated formatting that can do the hard work for you.

It's an unfortunate truth that most writing apps don't do paperback formatting well at the time of this writing. Unless you use a dedicated formatting app, there's no guarantee that your book will look professional unless you spend a lot of time tweaking your file.

My recommendation is to use a dedicated formatting app if you can. You'll bypass the frustration that many new authors experience with paperback formatting. Many people underestimate how challenging it is.

For Mac, your best bet is Vellum—it will generate beautiful e-books and paperbacks every time, and it's easy to learn.

Windows users don't have the same luck. Atticus is your best bet because it's browser-based. It offers much of the same functionality as Vellum. Otherwise, you'll have to resort to Microsoft Word or Adobe InDesign. Microsoft Word is notoriously difficult for paperback formatting and Adobe InDesign is notoriously expensive (and it has a difficult learning curve).

Linux users have it the worst of all. I would recommend Atticus for their paperback formatting needs.

It's also worth mentioning that Draft2Digital also offers a free paperback formatting tool.

Choosing a dedicated formatting app frees up your flexibility to choose whatever writing app you like without having to worry about formatting. For example, if being able to format paperbacks is one of your deal breakers, but you really like the simplicity of Markdown apps, you can still purchase the Markdown app and not have to worry about it.

In the previous chapter when discussing e-book formatting, we discussed the two essential elements of a properly formatted book: utility and ease of navigation.

For a paperback, utility is important. For example, an appropriate font, a proper font size (usually 11-point), and a trim size that's comfortable to hold comprise a paperback's utility.

For a paperback's navigation, a table of contents is important (more so for nonfiction), but so are page numbers and headers so readers know where they are at all times.

Keep this in mind as you shop for writing apps with paperback formatting functionality.

Things to Look For

Writing apps with paperback formatting functionality should allow you to customize:

1. trim size (length and width)
2. margins and gutters
3. running headers and footers
4. widow and orphan control

These topics are beyond the scope of this book. I share them merely to bring it to your attention and to make it clear that if an app does not allow you to customize these items, then it does not offer *true* paperback formatting.

The final element to consider is images. I mentioned in the last chapter that images and e-books don't always get along. The same is true with paperbacks. You'll need to follow your paperback retailer's image guidelines so that your images are formatted properly. Some writing apps can insert images into your paperback, for example, but they don't offer the ability to use full-bleed images that take up an entire page. You may also want to wrap text around an image or make it circular instead of rectangular. You may struggle with this outside of a dedicated formatting app.

Finally, there may be some front and back matter pages that you want in your e-book but not in your paperback, and vice versa. If this is something you need, then be sure to evaluate your writing app accordingly.

Paperback formatting is hard, but it's not impossible. If you choose to do it within your writing app, cultivate patience and an experimental mindset and you'll succeed.

BACKING UP YOUR WORK

Backing up your work is important. Your words are data, and data is susceptible to life.

For example, you may accidentally spill coffee on your computer, ruining it. Or, your house might burn down, destroying your computer. Or, you might be the victim of a ransomware or cyberattack. Or, your computer's hard drive might fail. Anything can happen.

Writing app developers have recognized this and have implemented several features to protect your data so that you won't lose your manuscript even if disaster strikes.

Auto-Save

Auto-save saves your manuscript every few seconds so that you don't have to remember to click the save button.

Microsoft Word's Auto-Save button. (Windows). View in high-resolution at www.authorlevelup.com/handbookimages.

Most of the major desktop apps have auto-save functionality and all browser-based apps I tested do. You won't find this on phone apps outside of Microsoft Word, however. But this space is ever-evolving and anything can change at any time.

Versioning

Versioning is a commonly requested manual feature that lets you save a version of your work. For example, you may want to save a version of your project after each draft. Or, you may be in the middle of your story and are unsure where to go with the plot, so you save a version just in case you need to revert to it later.

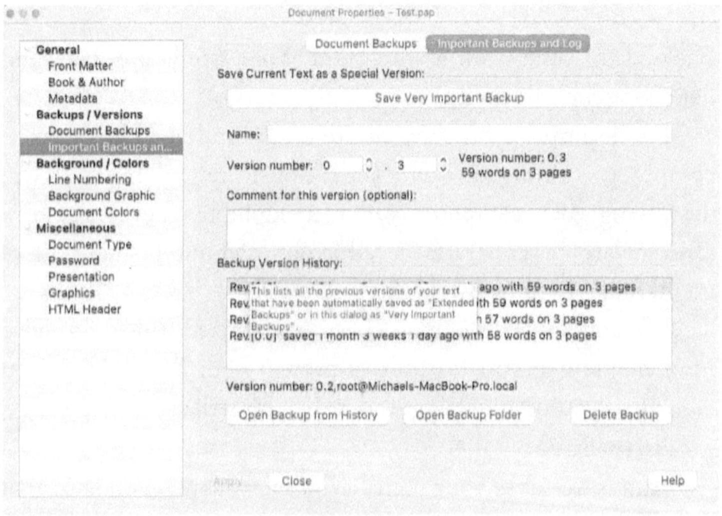

Versioning support in Papyrus Author. You can name each version. (Mac). View in high-resolution at www.authorlevelup. com/handbookimages.

Save a Version?

Storyist automatically saves versions (backup copies) of your project as you write. You can also create a version manually using this dialog. Versions created with this window are also available in the Versions browser.

Optional comment:

?   Cancel   Save a Version

Versioning support in Storyist. You can add optional comments for each version. (Mac). View in high-resolution at www.authorlevelup.com/handbookimages.

Scrivener is unique because it doesn't offer versioning at the project level, but it does offer a snapshots feature that lets you create versions at the chapter level.

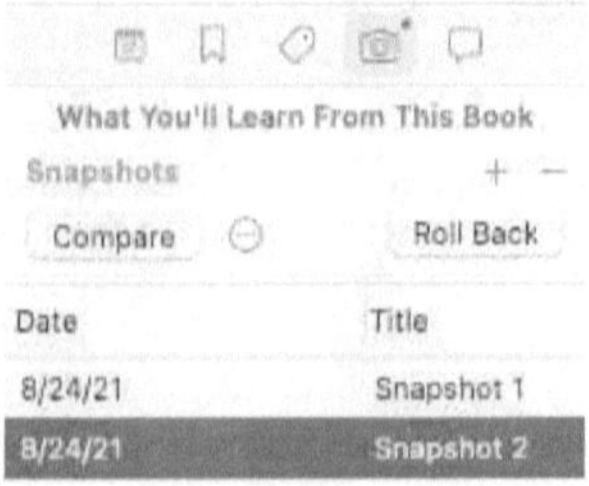
What You'll Learn From This Book
Snapshots
Compare
Roll Back
Date
Title
8/24/21
Snapshot 1
8/24/21
Snapshot 2

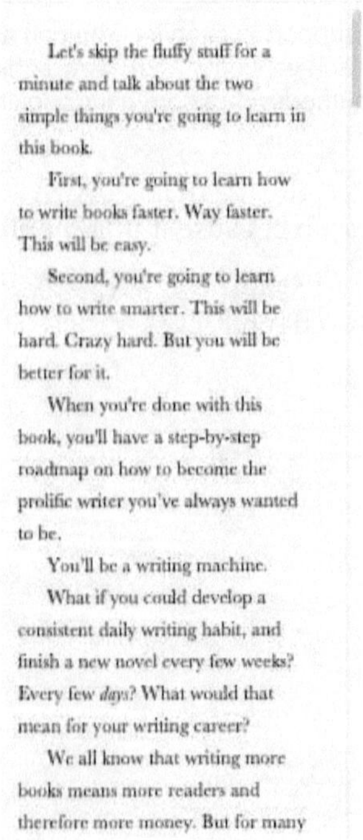
Let's skip the fluffy stuff for a minute and talk about the two simple things you're going to learn in this book.
First, you're going to learn how to write books faster. Way faster. This will be easy.
Second, you're going to learn how to write smarter. This will be hard. Crazy hard. But you will be better for it.
When you're done with this book, you'll have a step-by-step roadmap on how to become the prolific writer you've always wanted to be.
You'll be a writing machine.
What if you could develop a consistent daily writing habit, and finish a new novel every few weeks? Every few *days*? What would that mean for your writing career?
We all know that writing more books means more readers and therefore more money. But for many

Snapshots feature in Scrivener. (Mac). View in high-resolution at www.authorlevelup.com/handbookimages.

Automatic Backup

Some writing apps back up everything you do without you having to click a button. These apps usually back up your entire project at designated intervals, and if you ever need to find an old version, you can open up your backup folder and search for the version you need.

Those are the major ways that writing apps can back up your work. Even if you are careful, I guarantee you'll need to access a backed-up version of your work at least a few times in your writing career. You never hope you have to use it, but when you do, you'll be glad you had it.

THE HALL OF FAME: MOST INNOVATIVE WRITING APP FEATURES

In this section, I want to recognize the innovation of writing app developers. The features you're about to read about push writing apps forward and bring us closer to being the writers of the future.

The features I selected are only available in one writing app, maybe two. I believe they are major selling points. Again, I'm not endorsing anyone; I'm just giving credit where credit is due.

If you see a feature that resonates with you but the app itself isn't to your liking, write your developer. If enough people do that, we'll get some healthy competition going—and you might just get the feature you asked for!

ATTICUS: THE ALL-IN-ONE APPROACH

Atticus is a scrappy little app that launched in 2021 with a big goal: to be a one-stop-shop for every phase in the writing process.

You can write your novel in Atticus with its industry-standard browser-based word processor, which is smooth.

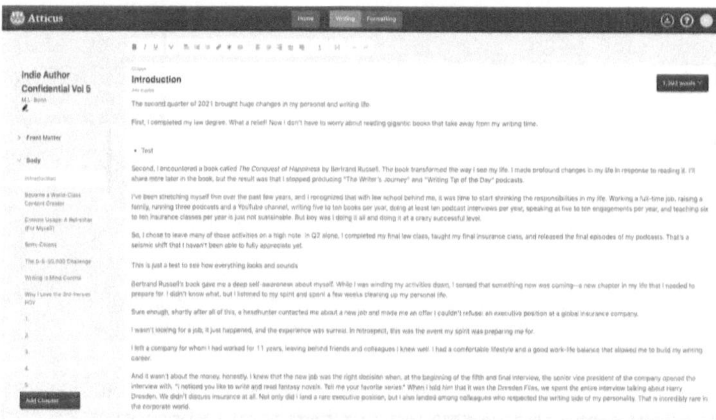

Atticus's Writing mode. (Web-Based). View in high-resolution at www.authorlevelup.com/handbookimages.

In a future release, you will be able to edit your novel in Atticus by granting your editor permission. They'll be able to log in to Atticus and edit your book within the app, and then you'll be able to review the changes. In an interview on the 20 Books Facebook group, the app's creator, Dave Chesson, aimed to make Atticus a primary way that editors do business, bypassing Microsoft Word (I'm paraphrasing him, but I believe I captured the spirit of his message). I unfortunately can't share a link to this interview, but hopefully, you trust me enough to relay his thoughts as I heard them.

When it's time to format your book, just click a button and Atticus goes into formatting mode, giving you an easy, beautiful interface similar to Vellum, where you can generate e-books and paperbacks editions in just a few minutes.

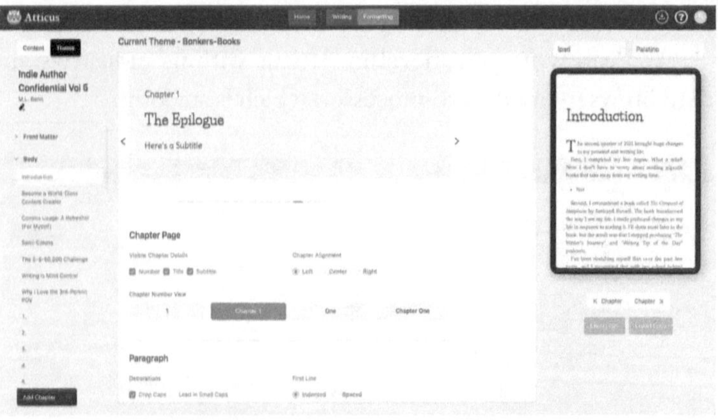

Atticus's Formatting mode. (Web-Based). View in high-resolution at www.authorlevelup.com/handbookimages.

Whether Atticus succeeds or fails, I can't help but applaud its innovative approach. If it succeeds, it's the closest thing we currently have to the writing app of the future. I predicted an app like Atticus almost two years before it was created—I predicted that an app that kept everything in one ecosystem could radically disrupt the writing app world as we know it. You can read about my predictions in the next section.

DABBLE WRITER: PROWRITINGAID INTEGRATION

I wrote previously about Dabble's ProWritingAid integration, which was innovative and one of those ideas that make you say, "Wow. How come no one else thought of this?"

They deserve more credit and a second mention! After all, if you use an advanced spelling and grammar app like ProWritingAid or Grammarly, why *wouldn't* you want to keep your manuscript within your writing app and just apply the advanced spelling and grammar checks there?

I hope more writing apps find a way to integrate spelling and grammar checkers like this.

GOOGLE DOCS: THE OG IN SIMULTANEOUS COLLABORATION

More authors are writing books together than ever before.

I co-wrote a series with my friend, Justin Sloan (Modern Necromancy). At the beginning of our collaboration, we traded Word documents back and forth via email. It was a disaster and, at one point, we lost chapters because we got mixed up, so we switched to Google Docs.

At the time of this writing, nothing beats Google Docs for simultaneous collaboration. Two or more people can work on the same document at the same time. Google Docs sets the standard for collaboration, but it is not designed specifically for writers.

Google really should be commended for the technology it created. Hopefully, someone else can replicate it.

PAPYRUS AUTHOR: TRACKED CHANGES

Papyrus Author offers tracked changes that are almost identical to Microsoft Word's. It is the only app I know of at the time of this writing that offers such a feature.

People have been asking for tracked changes in Scrivener for as long as I can remember, but it never happened. I've seen others request it from their favorite writing app developers, but to no avail.

The beauty of Papyrus Author is that you can import a manuscript with your editor's edits and then work on them within Papyrus Author. This means that the only thing you have to do is export your manuscript to Word so your editor can work on it. Except for that brief export and import, your book doesn't leave the Papyrus Author ecosystem.

SCRIVENER: ASSISTED FEATURE SEARCH

A major complaint from new Scrivener users is that the app has so many features that it's hard to remember where they are. It's not uncommon to spend time hunting in the menus until you find the feature you're looking for.

Mac users of Scrivener have benefited from Mac OS's assisted menu search for a while. When you search for a feature, the correct menu will collapse and an arrow will point to the feature. After a few times, you won't need to search for the feature anymore.

With the release of Scrivener 3 for Windows in 2021, Literature & Latte implemented the same feature into the Windows version. I've never seen a Windows app with a feature like this. It's a remarkable feature that helps the Windows version stay consistent with its Mac counterpart.

Windows and Mac users are lucky to have such a great search feature!

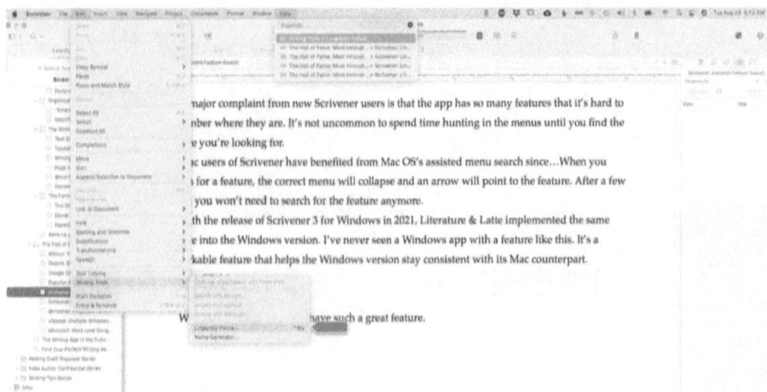

Scrivener's Assisted Search feature. (Mac). View in high-resolution at www.authorlevelup.com/handbookimages.

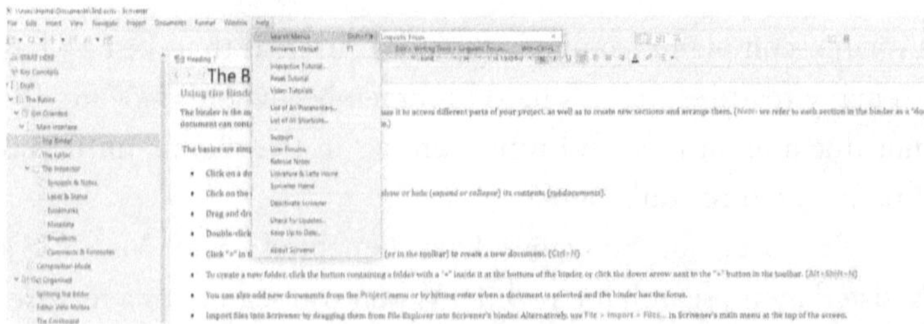

Scrivener's Assisted Search feature. (Windows). View in high-resolution at www.authorlevelup.com/handbookimages.

SCRIVENER: COMPOSITION MODE

Scrivener had a distraction-free mode before it was cool. And that distraction-free mode had a dark mode before it was cool too.

I'm of course referring to Scrivener's Composition Mode tool. Click a button and the app goes into full-screen mode, but there's a twist: the toolbar and binder disappear and what's left is a mutable page that you can adjust to suit your preferences. You can zoom in or out, modify the page width, and enter type-writer mode. You can even fade your desktop in and out around your page, or you can just rely on a dark background to help you focus.

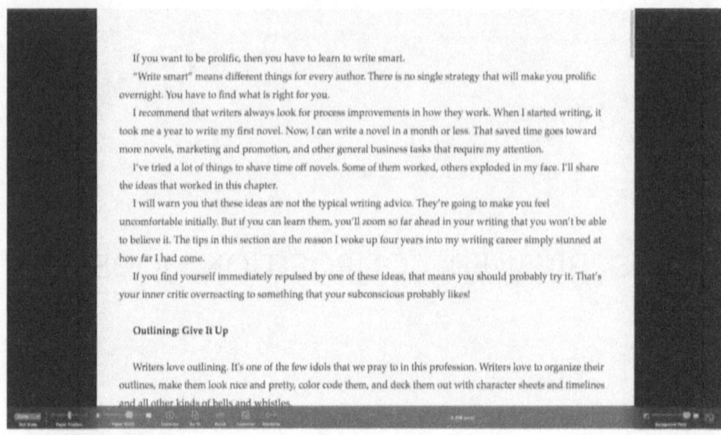

If you want to be prolific, then you have to learn to write smart.

"Write smart" means different things for every author. There is no single strategy that will make you prolific overnight. You have to find what is right for you.

I recommend that writers always look for process improvements in how they work. When I started writing, it took me a year to write my first novel. Now, I can write a novel in a month or less. That saved time goes toward more novels, marketing and promotion, and other general business tasks that require my attention.

I've tried a lot of things to shave time off novels. Some of them worked, others exploded in my face. I'll share the ideas that worked in this chapter.

I will warn you that these ideas are not the typical writing advice. They're going to make you feel uncomfortable initially. But if you can learn them, you'll zoom so far ahead in your writing that you won't be able to believe it. The tips in this section are the reason I woke up four years into my writing career simply stunned at how far I had come.

If you find yourself immediately repulsed by one of these ideas, that means you should probably try it. That's your inner critic overreacting to something that your subconscious probably likes!

Outlining: Give It Up

Writers love outlining. It's one of the few idols that we pray to in this profession. Writers love to organize their outlines, make them look nice and pretty, color code them, and deck them out with character sheets and timelines and all other kinds of bells and whistles.

Scrivener's Composition Mode. The app's menus disappear, replaced by a more simplistic menu at the bottom that is only visible if you hover over it with your mouse. (Mac). View in high-resolution at www.authorlevelup.com/handbookimages.

Composition Mode even has a Focus Mode that spotlights the current sentence or paragraph you're working on to help you concentrate even more.

If you exit Composition Mode to Scrivener proper, the app will save your settings so that your next session in Composition Mode will be consistent.

It's a very strong feature that I wish more apps tried to emulate.

SCRIVENER: LINGUISTIC FOCUS

Whenever I demo Scrivener for audiences, Linguistic Focus wows the crowd. It's the earliest potential use of artificial intelligence in a writing app that I know of. (This is speculation on my part, but I'm fairly certain that this is in fact an AI tool.)

The concept behind Linguistic Focus is simple: select certain parts of speech and then fade out the rest so that you can focus solely on the parts you've selected. This way, you can focus on certain parts of your text in isolation, which makes it easier for you to spot errors.

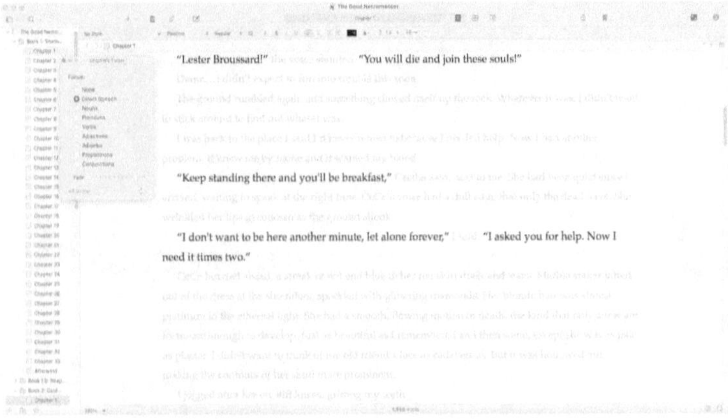

Scrivener's Linguistic Focus (known as Dialogue Focus on Windows). The dialogue is full black, with everything else faded to gray to help the user see the dialogue better. The Mac version supports additional parts of speech to focus on. (Mac). View in high-resolution at www.authorlevelup.com/handbookimages.

At the time of this writing, the Mac version of Scrivener supports almost every part of speech. The Windows version only supports dialogue.

Linguistic Focus is an amazing accomplishment. Let's take a moment to appreciate (at a high level) what the developers had to do to pull this off.

1. They needed a way to tag every word in the English language (nouns, verbs, adjectives, and so on). This is not easy. I believe they accomplished this through open-source work that's already been done by leading universities in natural language processing (NLP), which is a form of artificial intelligence. They probably also used the famous Natural Language Toolkit (NLTK) somehow.

2. They needed to find a way to highlight the chosen parts of speech and then fade out everything else.
3. Whatever the level of fade, it has to be non-destructive; meaning just because it disappears doesn't mean it's truly gone.

The result is a masterful feature that is a wonder of modern writing apps. Maybe I'm completely wrong about how Literature & Latte built it; maybe it's much simpler than it lets on. But if that's true, you have to wonder why other apps haven't done something similar.

ULYSSES: MULTIPLE WINDOWS AND TABS AT THE SAME TIME

In the previous section, I discussed the ability to write in multiple tabs and/or windows. This is a relatively common feature on desktop writing apps, but no app does it quite like Ulysses.

Ulysses lets you write in multiple tabs *and* windows at the same time. Each window of Ulysses is a separate instance of the app.

For example, I have dual monitors. On my primary monitor, I can have two Ulysses windows open and use the snap assist feature so that they both take up half the screen. Then, I can divide each of those windows with tabs.

On my secondary monitor, I can do the same thing!

And best of all, Ulysses handles it well and there's no sacrifice in performance.

I love this feature because you can treat windows like napkins. Just discard them when you're done, and everything gets saved properly.

ULYSSES: STYLE EXCHANGE

Ulysses is perhaps the most aesthetically customizable writing app on the market. Not only does it support light and dark modes, but it supports color palette customizations too. Through its theme exchange, users can create *and* download styles that work best for their personalities. No color combination is out-of-bounds. If you want a yellow color palette, go for it! A palette that reminds you of a Caribbean beach? Yep.

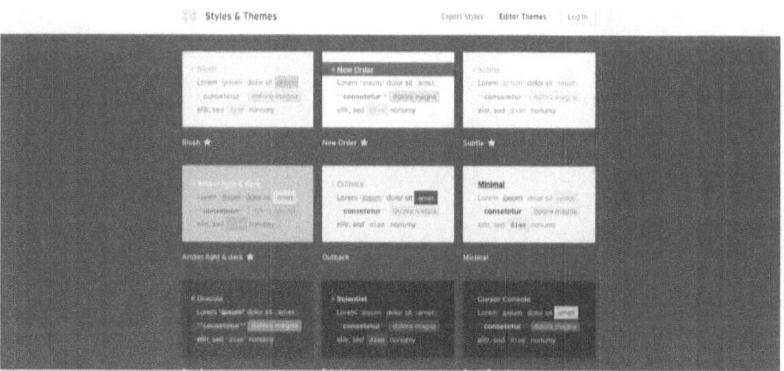

An image of Ulysses's theme exchange website. View in high-resolution at www.authorlevelup.com/handbookimages.

I love the flexibility. While other writing apps offer color themes, Ulysses goes above and beyond. It has a certain level of ease and a cool factor that can't be beaten at the time of this writing. Users are always submitting new themes, and the Ulysses team curates them on the theme website. The themes are shockingly easy to install as well. Just download and click.

MICROSOFT WORD (AND GOOGLE DOCS): MACROS

When it comes to efficiency, no app does it better than Microsoft Word's macro feature.

A macro is a series of commands that the app executes for you automatically. It's a time saver. You can create macros with the macro recorder or by learning the Visual Basic for Applications (VBA) programming language. For this reason, many people avoid macros because they seem complicated. They can be, but they don't have to be.

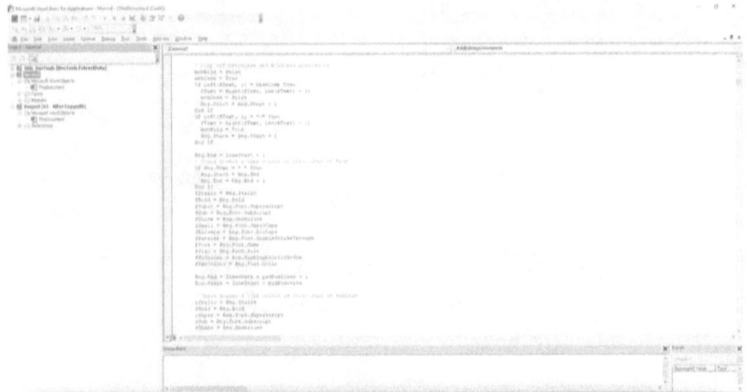

Microsoft Word macro code behind the scenes. (Windows).
View in high-resolution at www.authorlevelup.com/
handbookimages.

An entire industry of programmers has sprung up around VBA. Many people make a great living writing VBA code. That's how universal it is. You can hire a VBA programmer for cheap on a site like Fiverr for simple tasks.

Most people have heard of Microsoft Excel macros, but Microsoft Word's macro functionality is almost identical to Excel's, and it's very helpful in the editing process.

Paul Beverley created a free macro suite with hundreds of macros to help you catch errors in your work. I recommend that you check out his macros and watch videos on his YouTube channel to see what you can do with them. It will surprise you. You can learn more at https://www.archivepub.co.uk.

Google Docs also has robust macro support.

When you understand just how powerful macros can be, you will not want to get rid of Microsoft Word, even if the writing app of the future keeps everything within its ecosystem. Word is worth having just to be able to use macros in certain situations.

THE WRITING APP OF THE FUTURE: WHAT FEATURES WILL IT HAVE?

All of the writing apps I have spotlighted in this book have been fantastic, but are they the future of the writing app as know it?

Probably not.

I wrote about "the writing app of the future" in my *Indie Author Confidential* series, where I journal the lessons I'm learning on my writing journey. I like to write about technology in hopes that someone will read it and implement my ideas one day.

In the following passage, I offered my thoughts on the writing of the future:

The writer of the future needs a unified command center. Not a writing app, a formatting app, a spelling and grammar app, and the myriad other software we use.

My workflow today is as follows: I write my books in Scrivener, then export them to Microsoft Word so that my editor can edit using track changes. I review the editor's edits in Microsoft Word, run the manuscript through ProWritingAid, copy/paste the book back into Scrivener, then export to Vellum for formatting.

I despise the workflow, but it's the best we have right now.

It's unreasonable to expect one app to execute on the level of Scrivener, Microsoft Word, ProWritingAid, *and* Vellum, but it is reasonable to ask that the writing apps of the future work together seamlessly.

I'd like to write my novel in Scrivener and be able to send it to my editor, perhaps by granting the editor permission to edit my Scrivener file with tracked changes (if Scrivener ever supports that). Preferably, I should never have to leave my writing app for anything, even formatting.

The bestselling writing apps on the market are extremely vulnerable to disruption. Writers just don't realize it because the writing app as we know it hasn't changed in forty years and we can't conceive of how it can evolve.

If a new writing app functioned similarly to how I describe the following narrative, it would render the current landscape of writing apps irrelevant. Let's call it Shapeshifter.

Shapeshifter is a writing app that offers an interchangeable interface that supports WYSIWYG (what you see is what you get) writing interface a la Microsoft Word, or a Markdown experience like Ulysses. With one click, you can change its appearance and therefore its layout. It's two or three different writing apps in one. That's the app's headlining feature. It "shapeshifts" extremely well, molding itself to suit the writer instead of asking the writer to adapt to it.

The desktop version is available on Windows and Linux. Mac users were originally left out, but they quickly learned that they could run the app by installing Windows on their computers—a deliberate and intelligent choice on the developers' part that allowed them to seize the Windows market, which was ripe for a new, modern competitor. Given the benefits you're about to hear, Mac users will have no qualms about upgrading their computers to quickly abandon their current writing app. Ironically, the app is available on iOS, iPad OS, and Android, with good feature parity so that users can write on the go no matter their phone or tablet.

Shapeshifter is also available in the browser, with an optimized writing experience.

No matter where you are or what device you are using, Shapeshifter will shift to suit your preference.

If that were it, Shapeshifter would be remarkable. But here's what makes it the writing app of the future: out of the box, the app itself is not terribly robust. It has a few key features such as a word processor and the ability to import and export.

However, the app has way more features available; you purchase what you need. If you don't need a distraction-free mode, you don't have to pay for it. If you ever want it, you pay a onetime fee of $5. The app and its features are like LEGOs that you can snap together based on your preferences. Every writer's app will look different; in fact, writers are encouraged to share their "space," which is linked to a generous affiliate program that rewards them for every referral they make.

Shapeshifter is also the first writing app other than Microsoft Word to offer third-party developer integration. The app's in-house features are comparable to most other writing apps, and without any integrations, it looks rather vanilla. Third-party integrations are where the app shines. Developers can create new kinds of writing tools—outlining features, dictation support, macros, and integration with other apps, like voice assistants. All of these plugins help you become a better version of yourself. This also allows the app to stay at the forefront of advancements in operating systems.

Shapeshifter offers a Discord or a Reddit community where users can request new plugins and developers can create them.

The app gathers a cult following that quickly becomes mainstream.

Now, let's talk about the biggest selling point: the price.

Shapeshifter's developers wanted to create an affordable writing app and avoid the ire of the community by switching pricing models. For a onetime fee of $30, you pay to own the app. The developers keep the prices low because you pay à la carte for additional features such as cloud syncing between mobile and desktop and WordPress blog integration, for example. You only pay for the features you'll use. Overall, you might pay around $200-300 over the lifetime of the app, more including plugins, which can range from a couple of dollars to a few hundred dollars, depending on the plugin.

And that's not all...

Shapeshifter is just one app in a suite of apps for writers. Shapeshifter Writer handles the writing. You see, the developers figured out that it's impossible to do everything well in one app, so they modeled their app suite after the Adobe Creative Cloud so that all their apps work together seamlessly.

Shapeshifter Writer is an app and marketplace for *writing*.

When it's time to edit, the writer can, with the click of a button, "shift" the app into Editor mode, which is technically a separate application in its own right that you can also purchase.

Editor is optimized for editing. Shapeshifter Editor is a pioneering editing app that is designed solely for the back-and-forth between a writer and editor. Drawing inspiration from apps like Google Docs and Asana, a writer and editor can collaborate on a manuscript without the manuscript ever leaving the Editor ecosystem. All the author has to do is invite the editor to join a given project. The editor can edit the book in a browser and does not need to purchase the software, though doing so under an Editor's license will grant them unique benefits.

All edits that the author accepts in Editor get pushed to Writer so that the manuscript is in sync everywhere. The author can of course revert and roll back changes at any time.

Editor also supports third-party integration, such as Grammarly, ProWritingAid, and anything else a developer can dream of in the editing process. Editor would also encourage and support artificial intelligence plugins.

When it's time to format your manuscript, you can "shift" to Shapeshifter Formatter with the click of a button. With just one click and a smooth wizard, you can have a publish-ready e-book and print edition. It offers the power of Vellum but also third-party integration for formatting templates and special features such as indexes. You could even grant access to a formatter who could upload HTML that the app would accept. Changes you make in Formatter are automatically synced with Writer and Editor.

Formatter even integrates with book retailer APIs so you can publish without having to leave the app.

Shapeshifter's holy triumvirate of Writer, Editor, and Formatter succeeds because it streamlines the process of writing and helps writers do more in less time. It takes advantage of the fact that some writing apps go years without receiving updates as well as writers' frustration with subscription-based apps. It leverages the power of Adobe-smooth integration between the three apps, with the ease of use and customization of Reaper (a very popular sound-recording app among musicians).

While the future of writing apps may look different from the narrative I've written, consider that writing apps as we know them haven't changed much in forty years as I mentioned earlier. With emerging technology, writers will have such a need to evolve that it will be a no-brainer if someone offers them the ability to move to the cutting edge of technology and writing.

I wrote this article in 2020, but I was talking about the concept on my podcasts as early as 2019.

Most of the predictions I made haven't come true yet, but Atticus certainly is taking the all-in-one approach that I wrote about. If you liked any of the ideas you read, share them.

INTEGRATIONS

Integrations are a fairly new trend at the time of this writing, but it's worth knowing about.

Most writing apps are closed ecosystems. This means that everything you can access is within the writing app.

There is such a thing as an open ecosystem: Microsoft Word. You can download or buy a wide variety of third-party plugins that you can access in the ribbon. Two easy examples are Grammarly and ProWritingAid—both offer very good integrations with Word.

Word is peerless in this area. I'm starting to see writing apps develop a semi-closed ecosystem where some integrations are allowed.

For example, Ulysses offers seamless integration with WordPress, Medium, and Ghost. You can publish posts without having to leave Ulysses. You can even schedule posts in the future and even update existing blog posts that you already published!

Another honorable mention is Dabble Writer, which offers integration with ProWritingAid.

Whether a developer can create an integration is not always

within the developer's control, but I believe we'll see more integrations like these in the future.

FINAL THOUGHTS

The future is bright for writers. There has never been a better time to be an author.

We have access to more writing apps than ever before. Those apps are better than ever before, and affordable.

New emerging technologies such as artificial intelligence and blockchain are poised to forever change how we create stories and make money.

And most importantly, we have so much freedom in how we want to live our lives as writers.

I don't know about you, but that excites me. As someone who considers my writing apps extensions of my fingers, I can't wait to see what the future will hold, and I hope you do too.

I've taught you everything I know about writing apps. Now turn the page and learn about the free tool I developed to help you find your perfect match.

FIND YOUR PERFECT WRITING APP
WITH THIS FREE TOOL

I created a free tool designed to help you pick your perfect writing app in just a few clicks. It's called the Writing App Database.

You can filter and sort the database by the most important app features: operating system, e-book and paperback formatting, dark mode, and even price!

Check it out today at www.authorlevelup.com/writingapps.

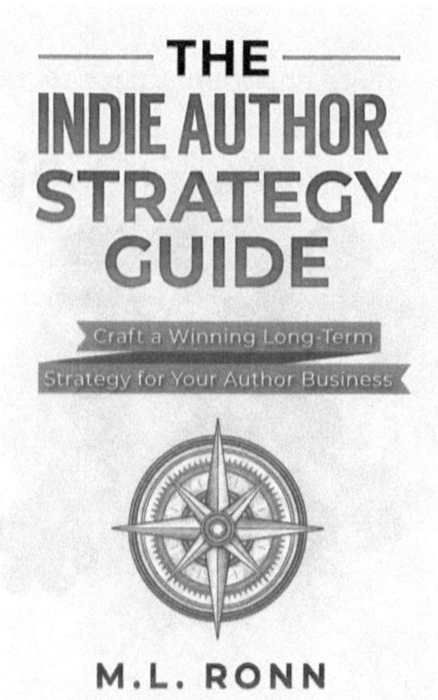

What's your author strategy?

Strategy is more than selling books. It's about the survival of your author career tomorrow, next year, 10 years from now, and beyond.

In this guide, prolific author M.L. Ronn will teach you how to cultivate the practice of long-term thinking and strategic planning. He draws on his experience of over a decade of self-publishing and extensive experience in the corporate world where strategic planning is his job.

In this guide, you'll learn:

- How to craft a winning author strategy that will make you look like an evil genius in retrospect
- How to think long-term
- What strategy is and what it isn't
- How to connect a bigger strategy to what you're doing every day to write and sell books

Few things are more important than a sound author strategy. Buy now to learn how to develop yours!

Get your copy today at www.authorlevelup.com/strategy.

MEET M.L. RONN

Science fiction and fantasy on the wild side!

M.L. Ronn (Michael La Ronn) is the author of many science fiction and fantasy novels including *The Good Necromancer*, *Android X*, and *The Last Dragon Lord* series.

In 2012, a life-threatening illness made him realize that storytelling was his #1 passion. He's devoted his life to writing ever since, making up whatever story makes him fall out of his chair laughing the hardest. Every day.

Learn more about Michael
www.authorlevelup.com (for writers)
www.michaellaronn.com (fiction)

Books for Writers

Indie Author Confidential (Series)
    How to Write Your First Novel
    Be a Writing Machine
    Mental Models for Writers
    The Indie Writer's Encyclopedia
    The Indie Author Atlas
    The Indie Author Bestiary
    The Reader's Bill of Rights
    The Self-Publishing Compendium
    150 Self-Publishing Questions Answered
    Authors, Steal This Book
    The Indie Author Strategy Guide
    How to Dictate a Book
    Advanced Author Editing
    Keep Your Books Selling
    The Author Estate Handbook
    The Author Heir Handbook

Interactive Fiction: How to Engage Readers and Push the Boundaries of Story Telling
Indie Poet Rock Star
Indie Poet Formatting
2016 Indie Author State of the Union

More Books for Writers:

www.authorlevelup.com/books

Fiction:

www.michaellaronn.com/books

www.ingramcontent.com/pod-product-compliance
Lightning Source LLC
Chambersburg PA
CBHW021144260726
48656CB00024B/1447